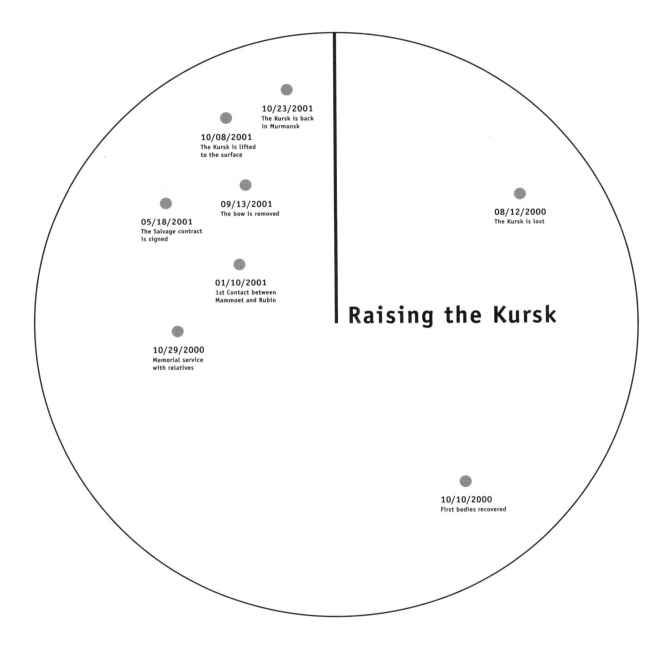

10/23/2001
The Kursk is back
in Murmansk

10/08/2001
The Kursk is lifted
to the surface

09/13/2001
The bow is removed

05/18/2001
The Salvage contract
is signed

08/12/2000
The Kursk is lost

01/10/2001
1st Contact between
Mammoet and Rubin

Raising the Kursk

10/29/2000
Memorial service
with relatives

10/10/2000
First bodies recovered

288
-03

2

T -0095.BH

PUBLICATION CREDITS

1st Print UK October 2004
Publisher Lipstick Publishing Tel: UK 01464 821954
ISBN 1-904762-05-0
Graphic Design Graphic Invention bv
Printing PlantijnCasparie Utrecht
Author Hans Offringa
Photography OWTV, Mammoet Archives, Maisterman-ItarTass Photo Agency,
Aad van Leeuwen, Hans de Jong, Wim v/d Hulst, Piet Sinke, Michel Bex
Illustrations Mammoet Archives, ANP, Bumblebee Studios, Joe Lertola
copyright 2001 Time inc.
Composition Hans Offringa and Larissa van Seumeren
English Translation Denis Campbell & Hans Offringa

DVD

Interviews in Russia Hans Offringa, Machiel Martens (camera),
Rogier Engels (sound)
Interviews in Scotland Hans Offringa, Machiel Martens (camera),
Ferry van Dingstee (sound)
Interviews in Holland Hans Offringa, Edwin Otter (camera),
Ferry van Dingstee (sound)
Editing Interviews Videoprofessionals V.O.F., Jelle Visser
Documentary OWTV
Computer Animation Bumblebee Studios
Translations Jelena Thijs, European Business Translations,
Denis Campbell & Hans Offringa

Sources
To describe the possible cause of the disaster I used information from the
book Lost Subs, by Spencer Dunmore, published by Madison Press Books.
The part about the Kursk Foundation is derived from articles published in
the Dutch newspapers NRC and De Volkskrant.

I wish to give thanks to all of those who gave us time and the opportunity
for interviews. Without these conversations it would not have been possible
to write this book. I owe special thanks to Rubin Company's Igor Spassky,
Victor Baranov and Igor Ovdienko for their special contributions, sincerity
and emotional involvement during the conversations in St. Petersburg, and
to Anna Skorokhodova. Without her simultaneous English translations it
would not have been possible to include the information and the interviews
from Russia in this book.

Hans Offringa, October, 2003. The moral rights of the Author have been asserted.

Contents

Part 1 - **The Story**

Chapter 1 – Rise and Fall

In 1901, a passionate group of Russian sailors meet. They all share the same dream... the Russian Navy is only complete if it has a submarine at its disposal.

The group makes their proposal and a first draft is given to the government and head of state Czar Nicholas II. The Czar is so enthusiastic about this initiative that he decides to create a design department that is given the assignment to build the first Russian submarine. The Rubin Company is born. Seven people start that same year designing and building.

"perestroika" of 1989 brings this growth to a halt and eventually leads to a large downsizing. Today, the slightly more than century-old Rubin employs 1,800 people. In 102 years, 1,000 submarines are built of which 200 are outfitted with nuclear weapons and some with nuclear reactor systems. Around 1980, Rubin begins construction of a revolutionary new submarine unequaled in speed, stealth, power, security and weapons capability, the Oscar II class, type SSGN or "nuclear guided missile submarine". In twelve years 14 of them are produced. Each is named after a famous battle in Russian military history.

after the village where Russian tank battalions in 1943 handed the Germans an important defeat.

The Kursk is 154 meters (505 feet) in length or about as long as two Boeing 747 jets parked nose to tail. With a self weight of 18,000 metric tons (39,700 pounds), together with the Cruiser Peter the Great, they are the showpieces of the Russian Navy. This is not just any submarine. It is powered by 2 nuclear reactors and can carry a vast number of torpedoes and cruise missiles. The outside skin has been specially reinforced with a rubber coating to remain invisible to enemy sonar systems. The skin construction is so strong that it can resist an enemy torpedo attack or contact with a sea mine. The silent design of the propeller screw remains a well-kept military secret. The Kursk is seen as almost unsinkable and is awarded the title "best submarine of the Northern fleet".

In the years of the Cold War, Rubin - part of the Russian Ministry of Defense - will grow into an enterprise of more than 4,000 employees. The

These submarines, primarily meant to fight against American aircraft carriers, are launched with Russia's Northern and Southern fleets. The Kursk is named

On August 10, 2000, the Kursk sails for an exercise on the Barentsz Sea under the command of Captain Gennady Lyachin. In the early afternoon of August 12th the Kursk finishes its first exercise, where it successfully launches several torpedoes.

Lyachin sends a radio message to the Supreme Commander of the squadron. He wants to conduct a second exercise and asks permission for this new launch. The message, and also the permission of the commander, is monitored by the USS Loyal from more than 200 nautical miles away.
Not long after that transmission, the Americans hear - instead of a launch – a short explosion. 134 Seconds later the explosion is followed by an enormous bang. Seismologists from Norway and England register both the first and the second explosion with a force of 1.5 and 3.5 on the Richter scale. The last explosion contains a force of 2 tons (4,400 pounds) of TNT.

The torpedo room of the Kursk is completely destroyed in the blast. Both explosions cause an enormous pressure wave that winds its way through the submarine. In the conning-tower, the captain and officers are immediately killed.

The bow compartment is nothing more than a crumpled mass of steel. The watertight seal between it and the other compartments can only partially stop the blast. Not long afterwards the Kursk lands with an enormous thud on the bottom of the Barentsz Sea, 110 meters under the water surface, at longitude 69.37 N and latitude 37.34 E.

As is later found, the two nuclear reactors in the sixth compartment have not been damaged, thanks to their own in-built security.

Following standard Russian military procedure, exercise reports need to be filed before 11:00 p.m. That hour passes with no message. The Kursk also does not respond to radio calls from Northern Fleet Headquarters. This starts an immediate search and rescue mission. Sunday morning the Peter the Great picks up a sonar contact of (as of that moment) an unknown ship lying on the bottom of the sea. This

cannot be any other vessel than the Kursk. Monday morning, August 14th, the Russian media are told that there are problems on board the submarine. Meanwhile an alarm has been struck by the fleet commander. The rescue mission fails. The second one also fails. 4 Days after the disaster on August 16, 2000, President Putin gives, from his holiday home, permission to seek rescue help from other foreign countries. A British rescue submarine leaves from Norway and arrives on Sunday, August 20th over the site of the sunken Kursk. The first attempt to open the escape hatch fails. A second attempt, by a pair of Norwegian divers, succeeds but unfortunately they see that the entire submarine is filled with water. An official announcement from Russia follows: "the crew of the Kursk has perished."

Then the floodgates of media criticism burst loose. The Russian Navy reacted too slowly and President

Putin made a big error of judgment by calling so late for help.

There is much speculation about the cause of the disaster. One first presumes there was a massive technical failure. Then the Russian government quoted directly from Minister Sergeyev that "the Kursk had a collision with an enemy ship on August 16th". Finally the statement comes that there was an explosion on board the submarine. Western experts are in agreement with that statement. Precisely what happened though remains unclear.

Above: Lt. Koleshnikov with his wife on the Kursk,

one month before the disaster.

Below: The farewell letter of Koleshnikov.

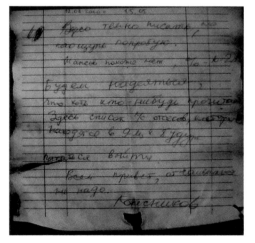

Much later, it is discovered that the Russian Navy used an experimental fuel, HTP (hydrogen peroxide) as an oxygenized heat source for a few of the torpedo motors. HTP by itself is not flammable, however, if it comes in contact with a catalyst, for example copper, it changes into oxygen and overheated steam which can expand in volume enormously and can cause the HTP holding containers to leak or explode. It could be that one of the containers was damaged on the Kursk and the build-up of pressure led to a chain reaction at the moment a torpedo was fired. In a German documentary, that was shown on television long after the accident, one can see one of the torpedoes breaking loose from its hanging sling during the loading of the Kursk and touching the wharf, which alone could have sown the seed for this terrible disaster. It remains quite speculative but the fact is that one-and-half years later, in February 2002, the Russian Navy started clearing this dangerous type of torpedo from their submarines. In that same summer Ilya Klebanov, the chairman of the inquest committee, announced that after long and comprehensive investigation it showed that the accident had not been caused by a sea mine or a collision. This confirms public opinion that a torpedo explosion inside the Kursk was the true cause of the disaster.

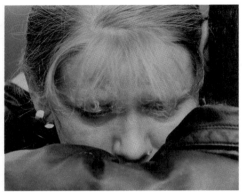

In October 2000, an attempt is made to salvage the bodies of the crew. The divers succeed and bring 12 bodies to the surface. Amongst them Captain Lt. Dmitri Koleshnikov. The salvage crew finds a farewell letter on his body. The short message is addressed to his wife and says that there are 23 crewmembers in the compartment, "none of us will be able to reach the surface", tells the last line of his macabre message. It must have been Hell for the crew during those last days. Wounded and becoming apathetic by the lack of oxygen and the knowledge they can't be saved anymore, the men one-by-one give up the ghost. It nevertheless remains an open question if faster action could have saved the lives of some of the crewmembers. It is generally assumed that after a couple of days nobody remained alive. Given the fact that the first attempt to open the escape hatches failed, that probably contributed to the cause. In the end, foreign help arrived 8 days after the disaster when it was almost certain no one was still alive.

On October 29, 2000, a memorial service is held in the Navy city of Severomorsk. The relatives are consumed with grief, in deep mourning and look for shelter against the snow behind the backs of the saluting guard of honor. President Putin has already promised to the Russian people that the Kursk will be salvaged. A big question remains: who will be allowed to do it?

Chapter 2 – The Assignment

of events leading up to the moment when Frans van Seumeren, Igor Spassky, Mikhail Barskov and Russian Vice President Klebanov on May 18, 2001 sign the salvage contract in the presence of scores of television cameras and journalists.

After hearing the first media stories about the loss of the Kursk a plan starts to develop in the mind of Jan van Seumeren. He thinks deeply about various methods to salvage the nuclear submarine and works out a couple of elementary drafts. At about the same time the chairman of the board of the salvage company Smit International, Nico Buis, picks up the telephone and activates his business network. While Jan is still drawing, Nico is building a strategy to bring in the salvage contract. Smit gets help from the Dutch government, a lobbying agency in Brussels and former political leaders.

A real Kursk Foundation is established with the goal of bringing European government subsidy money together to finance part of the salvage operation. One sees the accident as a European ecological disaster and wants to convince the member states that it is a good idea to jointly pay for the operation. The rest of the money will have to be put on the table by Russia. At the start this

Technically very complex, politically and militarily sensitive, with totally unpredictable weather circumstances on location and with two very different cultures that have to work together intensively for months. These are the ingredients for an assignment that seems to follow the company motto of Mammoet. "Welcome all difficulties" is the life maxim of founder Jan van Seumeren, Sr.; however, the enterprise doesn't get the assignment just like that. It is preceded by an historical series

Head-office Rubin at St. Petersburg.

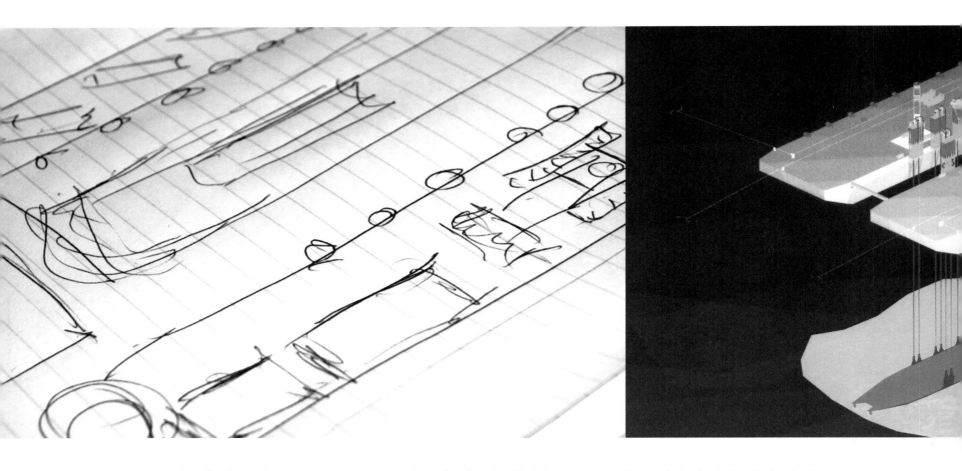

concept works well and soon there is € 223.500 available for a feasibility study to be executed by Smit. This plan is offered to the Russian Ambassador who gratefully exploits it. Meanwhile Smit has formed a consortium with the off-shore companies Heerema and Halliburton and is very busy working out a salvage method. The Russian government is enthusiastic about the plans for

partnership and co-financing. The Belgian salvage company Scaldis also manages to present a salvage plan to Rubin. Nothing as yet points to Mammoet, then still a completely unknown party in the maritime salvage business, that they could be a candidate for the contract. Jan and Frans van Seumeren are also make their moves. After a global plan has been worked out, Frans calls his office in

Moscow, in October 2000, with the directive to arrange a meeting with the Russian government. The first contacts are made by Slava Zakharov, director of Mammoet Russia. At first there is no reaction, until Zakharov manages to arrange a meeting to speak at Rubin in the beginning of January 2001. Coincidentally, Frans van Seumeren, his wife and a couple of friends are visiting

Left to right: Leo Versluis, Jan Kleijn and Wessel Helmens discuss several scenarios.

Moscow at that time. They immediately leave for St. Petersburg. The engineers of Rubin listen attentively to the presentation of Van Seumeren. However, after the presentation, Igor Spassky lets it be known that there is already a preliminary agreement with the consortium of Smit/Heerema/ Halliburton.

If Mammoet wants to join, the best way is to contact this group to see if there are any sub-contracts available. Van Seumeren says a friendly farewell to the gentlemen and travels back to Holland, slightly disappointed. At Mammoet the drawings of Jan van Seumeren disappear into the company archives. They do not as yet know that the Kursk Foundation is neither funded nor getting off to a good start.

The reasons are: the European Commission does not want to make the necessary funds available. In Brussels, political voices raise to tie the granting of these subsidies to an agreement with Russia to cleanup its nuclear waste in the Polar region. The ministry of Economic Affairs also does not consent in granting a loan guarantee for the Smit/Heerema/ Halliburton joint venture.

ФЕДЕРАЛЬНОЕ ГОСУДАРСТВЕННОЕ УНИТАРНОЕ ПРЕДПРИ

РУБИН

ЦЕНТРАЛЬНОЕ 191119, Россия
КОНСТРУКТОРСКОЕ Санкт-Петербург, ул. Мар
БЮРО Телефон /812/ 113
МОРСКОЙ ТЕХНИКИ Телефакс /812/ 164
E-mail: neptun@ckb-rubin.s

08.05.2001 № РУК/9-17
На № _____ от _____

Central Design Bureau for Marine Engineering Rubin, (further called the Client), hereby confirms its irrevocable intent to award Mammoet Company (the Netherlands),(further called the Executor), the contract for the heavy lift and transportation to the dock the submarine Koursk on the following agreed understandings:

The total agreed price for the works is 62 500 000,00 $ (Sixty two million and five hundred thousand US dollars) for the agreed scope of work and conditions as per protocol with the reference number N K –070 dated 08/05/2001.
Both parties undertakes their best efforts to sign the formal contract not later than 18th of May 2001.
Pending finalization and signing of the final contract the Executor is hereby authorized by the Client to start the work in accordance with this letter of intent and in line with the above mentioned protocol. These works will be paid by the Client to the Executor and included in the above mentioned total lumpsum price.

On behalf of the Client   On behalf of Executor

Mr. Spasski I.D.   Mr. Jan van Seumeren
General designer   Director
Head of the Bureau

Picture insert: The "famous" letter of intent.

When the Russian Foreign Minister Ivanov, in the first half of April, 2001, also lets his Dutch colleague Minister van Aartsen know that the salvage of the Kursk is not very high on his priority list, political support for the Kursk Foundation disappears.

Smit/Heerema/Halliburton want to begin their salvage preparations, as the window of time is beginning to press on them. If one wants to raise the Kursk in 2001, it has to be done in August. After that date the weather on the Barentsz Sea is very unpredictable. The negotiations over the financing cause such a delay that the consortium decides that 2001 will be the preparation year and 2002 the salvage year. This absolutely does not fit into Rubins plans, especially since President Putin has promised the Russian people that the Kursk,

with its crew, will be salvaged in 2001. The Russians gradually become fed-up with the political wrangling over subsidies and begin to investigate if they themselves can finance the entire operation.
Igor Spassky of Rubin smells trouble and quietly contacts Mammoet Moscow. Under the shroud of deepest secrecy Frans van Seumeren flies to St. Petersburg on the 16th of April. He is met at the airport and taken by personal escort directly to the offices of Rubin where he slips into a meeting with the top managers of Rubin and several high ranking military leaders of the Russian Navy. There he learns that the consortium both does not want and is not able to carry out the salvage operation in 2001.

Later Frans van Seumeren would say about that: "During the meeting it became quickly clear that

there were problems with the consortium and the Kursk Foundation. In my opinion that was caused by five factors.

First, the relationship between the Russians and the American-Dutch consortium was very frosty. This was caused by poor communications and the continual tug-of-war on the consortium side. This caused the people on the Russian side to become more and more nervous about whether the operation would begin on time as promised by President Putin to the Russian people.

Second, the role of the Kursk Foundation was a farce. They dangled the Russians a sausage in front of their noses that could not be eaten and Spassky and his people only discovered that later.

Ref. No K-169

To   MAMMOET
Attn   Mr. Frans van Seumeren

Fax   8/10/31-306695375

Re: **Kursk Recovery Project**

Dear Mr. Frans van Seumeren,

In accordance with your request I hereby confirm that there are no nuclear weapons aboard the Kursk submarine, which you will be lifting under the Contract No.07510551/01-01/BC dtd 18.05.2001.

Deputy Naval Commander-in-Chief
Vice-Admiral   M.K.Barskov

The letter stating there are no nuclear warheads on board the Kursk.

Third, there were, on the Russian side, problems with the payment guarantees. In my opinion, the American-Dutch consortium wanted a complete guarantee. From my experience I know that something like that is a very difficult and expensive case to make in Russia.

Fourth, the legal jurisdiction under which contract disputes would fall played an important role. The gentlemen were not agreeing on that one.

Last: my many years of experience with Russia have taught me that an emotional bond for Russians is of essential significance. We are and remain a family company and also maintain that atmosphere and feeling in our business dealings. For American and Western European companies that is often hard

to understand. A relationship there is often based on immediate business success and there is less "feeling out" to see if the person they do business with, is a man of conviction who stands for what he promises and gives himself for the full 100%.

Spassky told me later that he personally went to President Putin and said, "If we want to get the Kursk up in this year, we can only do it with Jan and Frans van Seumeren at Mammoet".

These points for me were merely suppositions in that first conversation. They became crystal clear during the actual negotiations."

And then the real negotiations started. Jan van Seumeren leaves for St. Petersburg, together with his left and right hand men Wessel Helmens and

Klaas Lamphen along with a pile of first drafts, detailed drawings and calculations. For 3 days there are talks, discussions, philosophical debates and thinking. On one side of the table sits the Dutch triumvirate, on the other side a 25-headed delegation of Russian engineers and in the middle 3 translators. This deliberation will eventually form the basis for the trust between both companies.

Over the next couple of days there is a lot of faxing, mailing and telephone calls to Holland. The Russian engineers questions are immediately answered by a team of engineers in the former Mammoet head office in De Meern. The Russians become impressed with the quick reaction capabilities of the people of Mammoet, while the Dutch gain more and more respect for the high knowledge level within Rubin.

Frans van Seumeren and Admiral Barskov answering the many

questions fired at them during a press conference in Moscow.

Russian Vice President Klebanov showing

the chosen lifting method to the press.

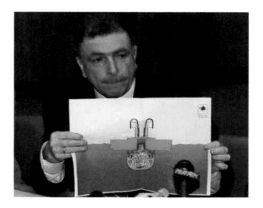

Reasonably quickly there is an agreement about the salvage method. Contained therein are a couple of innovations that Jan van Seumeren does not want to give away for free. That is why he asks Rubin for a letter of intent. With this precious document the triumvirate flies back the next day to Holland where Frans van Seumeren already has given the assignment to Leo Versluis and Jan Kleijn to start claiming production capacity at their two main sub-contractors. Nearly 5,000 tons (11,025 pound) of steel has to be formed into salvage equipment with only three months preparation time for engineering, design and... building.

The letter of intent forms a good starting point but it is not a contract yet. Over that, much heavy negotiation still must take place. This is not a simple affair, because in addition to Rubin and Mammoet the Russian ministries of Defense, Finance and Foreign Affairs, as well as the Federation of Russian Navy Shipyards are all involved in this matter. The negotiations are hard and Mammoet is assisted by experts from ABN-AMRO, AON Insurance and the British law firm Norton Rose, who specializes in maritime operations law. During the contract negotiations in St. Petersburg, the already time-squeezed engineering

processes continue to be worked on in the De Meern head office and options are taken on production capacity. This causes rumors to run wild throughout the market because there are very few salvage assignments that need as much material as Mammoet is planning to order. Smit International awakens with all this market activity and Nico Buis calls Frans van Seumeren. His suspicions are right and he offers his company's help on the maritime side where Mammoet has little experience. Van Seumeren induces Buis to a back-to-back agreement. In other words, Smit agrees even before the agreements Mammoet still has to make with Rubin are finalized. They create a joint venture because Smit is such a good sport that it is willing to also share the projects risk. Mammoet will place 70 per cent of the final contract in this temporary venture. They further decide to use the Norwegian diving firm DSND as subcontractor for all diving work. As it happens, DSND was already involved in the negotiations between Rubin and Mammoet. The diving ship "Mayo" has been reserved for the entire salvage operation. On the 18th of May the contract is signed: first the heavily damaged nose of the Kursk will be sawed off. After that the submarine will be lifted by a pontoon onto which stand 26 computer-operated

lifting units with heave compensation systems to neutralize the swell of the turbulent Barentsz Sea. To fasten the hull grippers, 26 holes have to be cut into the skin of the Kursk. When the Kursk is lifted and pulled up against the pontoon, it has to be tugged to the Bay of Murmansk where it will be placed in a gigantic dry-dock. The total contract bid is accepted for $65,000,000 dollars. There can be no more misunderstanding or negotiation about either the salvage method or the amount of money involved.

However, there are still 3 points where agreement has not yet been reached: the payment method, the insurance and the jurisdictional law under which the contract will be enforced. For this a separate appendix is drawn up with a contingency clause that cancels the deal if parties cannot reach a definitive agreement.

A week later Frans van Seumeren and Igor Spassky figure out the solution to these obstacles. Mammoet gives the Russians a bank guarantee of $16,000,000. Rubin subsequently makes a down payment of $16,000,000. The rest of the total contract amount will be paid into a special bank account in Holland. The project is divided into 16 stages and the payment for each stage will be handled separately.

Also the insurance coverage is formalized. The Russian government though must declare there are no nuclear warheads on board the Kursk. If that is the case, the insurance company does not want to cover the nuclear risk, which means the personnel cannot be insured. The declaration from the government comes (see picture on page 31). Mammoet wants Dutch or English law to prevail

while Rubin wants to have a contract under Russian law. Swedish law finally offers an acceptable compromise for both parties. In Holland the salvage preparations proceed at full speed.

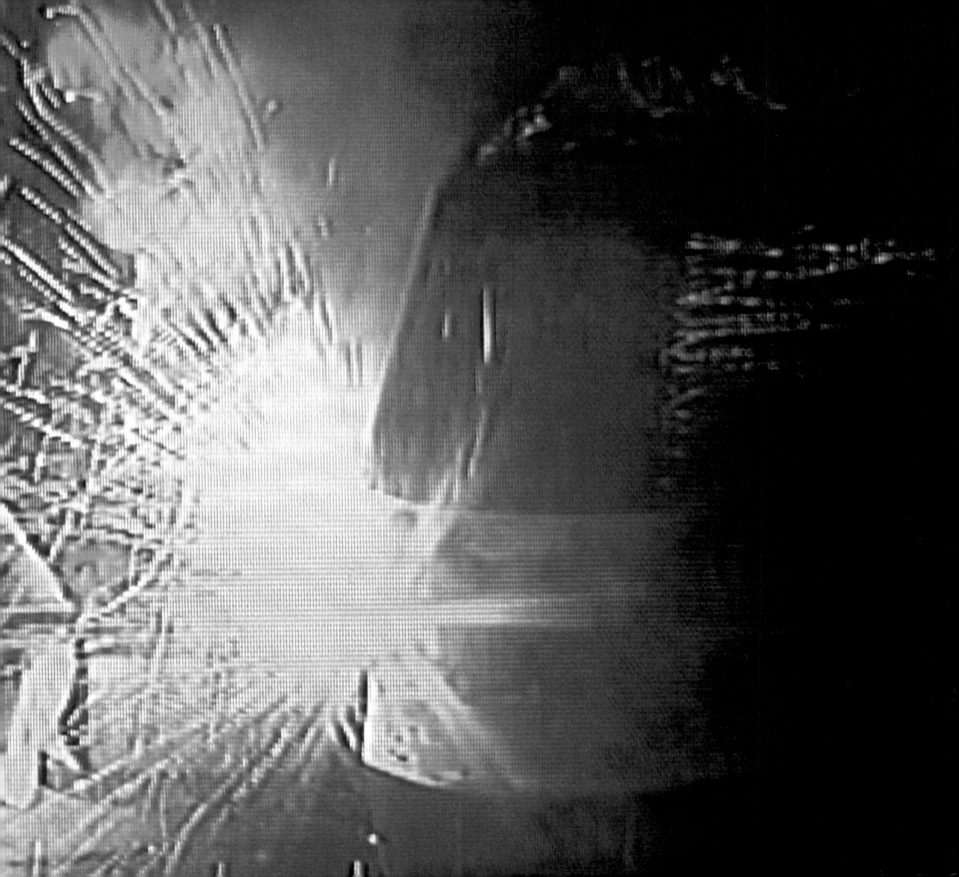

04:32:28

GIANT 4 24000TON
ROTTERDAM

Chapter 3 – The Preparations

In De Meern, the Mammoet head office has many people coming and going. Now that the contract is finalized, an entire floor is configured for use by all of the project specialists in the company. It is the nerve center of the whole operation. Leo Versluis is appointed the overall project manager. To him falls the complex task to successfully lead the gigantic logistic operation that precedes the actual salvage project. He appoints various sub-project managers for parts of the operation. Organizationally a myriad number of tasks must be arranged.

A joint venture is created with Smit International and everyone reaches agreement on the rough division of tasks. Mammoet focuses on the lifting activities and Smit focuses on the maritime operations. Officially the Ministry of Defense of the Russian Federation gives this assignment, but out-

sources that to the Rubin Company. Mammoet receives the assignment and places 70% of it in the joint venture that will be the main contractor for the various suppliers and sub-contractors. The Russians however, demand that Mammoet stay lead contractor and with that carry the full responsibility for the entire project. The remaining 30% Mammoet contracts out to: the Krylov Ship-building Research Institute which will perform a number of important tests, to ABN-AMRO for the financing and to the Russian state-owned company PO Sevmash, which takes on the responsibility for building the two large dry-dock pontoons as its assignment. With AON all insurance coverage is arranged in detail. In the joint venture the tasks of Mammoet and Smit are divided as follows: Mammoet performs the engineering work and also designs and builds the lifting platforms (winching

spools, strandjacks, heave compensation system, grippers and re-entry system), the complete computer steering system, the tests on all equipment and the lay-out of the saw and lifting pontoons. Smit concentrates on the maritime disciplines including: the diving vessel, the divers, the sawing, the cutting of the holes, the attachment of the grippers and other maritime activities (see the organizational chart on page 142).
Together with Frans van Seumeren, Leo Versluis creates a detailed planning and payment schedule. In this schedule the 16 stages of the project are shown, connected to all delivery deadlines and payment amounts (see schedule page 136-140).

The first stage is one of engineering, calculating and drawing. Not only all the complex pieces must be constructed but also all work procedures that

In three months time the Giant 4 transforms from a "bare floating hull" into a hi-tech lifting ship.

Testing of the scale model at the Krylov-Institute in St. Petersburg.

need to be followed are mapped and written out
in full detail.

The contribution of Rubin is essential. These Russian
engineers are better informed than anyone about
what can and cannot be accomplished. They are
the ones who designed and built the Kursk.
During this stage, there is already intensive contact
with supplier companies; the salvage method is
widely known, but most pieces of the salvage
equipment still need to be built.

The publicity in the press gives rise to many
potential suppliers simply contacting Mammoet
themselves. They are all eager to contribute a
"stone in the wall" to "the salvage of the century".
They also know that Mammoet is under a great
time constraint. The affect of this is that steel
prices rise. This means extra pressure on the internal

The start of pontoon dry-dock construction at the Russian Shipyard PO Sevmash.

The "landlubbers" of Mammoet prepare
themselves for a stay on the Barentsz Sea.

purchasing department at Mammoet, because they want to achieve the best price/quality ratio. However, they manage to reach agreements with the most important suppliers within 14 days. Already about 1,000 people are working on the preparation stages for the salvage. As time passes this number will grow to more than 2,000. The Mayo is reserved for the diving. Throughout the whole world, 75 experienced divers are approached and contracted. They will need to work continuously around-the-clock in 6-man teams during the salvage operation to blow the sand and silt away from the bottom around the sunken submarine, to saw off the Kursks nose and to cut the 26 holes and attach all grippers. Eventually about 125 men will work on the Mayo from where all underwater work will be executed and controlled under supervision of Mammoets Malcolm Dailey and DNSDs Wally Wallace.

The Norwegian company DSND is lined up for all of the underwater work.

A pontoon needs to be built up to transport the sawing installation to the Barentsz Sea. For that task the AMT carrier from England is tugged to Amsterdam. Constructed on the pontoon are a big crane, 2 enormous suction anchors, each more than 15 meters high (almost 50 feet), 3 hydraulic power packs and a sawing machine with chains.

The pontoon also must provide a home to a crew of 30 men. Reconstructed cargo containers will serve that purpose.

Finally the choice is made to use the pontoon Giant 4 as the lifting pontoon but it is absolutely not suited for that purpose in its current state. Normally the pontoon is used to transport cargo that lies on top of it. However, for this project the

"cargo" will hang underneath the ship. The Giant 4 is tugged to Amsterdam in the beginning of August, 2001 and is moored in a dock at Shipdock, Amsterdam. 26 holes are cut into its-130 meter (427 feet) long bottom. This procedure is carried out

following precise instructions of Rubins engineers because the positions of the holes in the Giant 4 have to exactly match the holes that will be cut into the hull of the Kursk. Grippers cannot be attached everywhere on the submarine since holes

The suction anchors on the sawing pontoon.

Sawing cable being tested.

The holes in the Giant 4;
on the Barentsz Sea the
grippers will be lowered
through them.

One of the saddles
under the Giant 4.

In the meantime, the company Hydrospex in Hengelo is busy building the cylinders for the heave compensation system and a couple of the strand- jacks. Piping Care and Van Bellum produce 26 nitrogen containers that will be attached to the system.

In Germany, IGH is modifying the computer software needed for the individual steering units of the heave compensation system.

In mid-August 2001 assembly of the 26 lifting platforms begins. Because all parts have to be assembled on location, on the grounds close to the Giant 4 a complete assembly area is built. Daily, from all over Europe, half-fabricated products are conveyed to the docking site.

cannot be cut into the compartments containing the nuclear reactors and cruise missiles.

These locations can be clearly seen in the illustration on fold-out page 19. Into the holes 26 pipes will be attached. Each pipe has a length of 15 meters (almost 50 feet) and a width of approximately 1 meter (3.2 feet). During the salvage operation, through each pipe 54 steel strands will be lowered. On each bundle of strands a gripper will be attached. The grippers are being built by the firm Huisman-Itrec, under the supervision of Arie de Zwart who has already played an important role in the design phase. Because the Kursk has to be pulled up snugly against the pontoon, it is also necessary to cut a big hole where the conning-tower of the submarine will

fit in. After cutting all of the holes the Giant 4 resembles a piece of Swiss cheese, but it still has to keep enough floating power to lift the 9,000 ton (20,162 pounds) heavy Kursk.

This is why deck reinforcements are built onto the pontoon where the lifting platforms with the strandjacks and the heave compensating systems will stand. In total there will be more than 5,000 tons of steel (5 million kilos!) (11 million pounds!) fitted onto the Giant 4. Under the pontoons big saddles are assembled that follow the rounded sides of the Kursk so that after lifting, the submarine can be tightly pulled against the Giant 4. On these saddles sit burls that will press into the rubber outside skin of the Kursk for a tight grip.

Construction of the 26 winching spools.

The strandjacks are being assembled and the cables spooled to the winching spools. Once the platform is ready, it will be hoisted aboard the Giant 4 with the help of a number of Mammoet cranes. Each lifting platform has a height of 15 meters (almost 50 feet), a weight of 60 tons (134,000 pounds) and consists of a strandjack (900 tons - 2 million pounds- lifting unit) with 54 strands (18 millimeter – 2/3 of an inch - thick steel cables each with a length of 140 meters – 459 feet), a spool that can winch the strands on and off so they don't take up space on the ships

Assembly and installation of the 26 lifting platforms.

Liquid Nitrogen

deck and 4 heave compensators, a kind of high tech shock absorber that will make sure that swell of the Barentsz Sea will be neutralized. Each heave compensation system has a maximum stroke of 3 meters (10 feet) and a diameter of 360 millimeters (14 inches). Lifting with strandjacks is a working method that has been successfully used by Mammoet for years. It is, however, the first time this method is to be used at sea. The spools and the heave compensation system are being pre-miered; these are complete new inventions of the Mammoet product development team that can only be tested live at sea.

To continuously provide the heave compensation system with nitrogen, 26 nitrogen containers, two containers with 7,000 litres (1,800 gallons) of liquid nitrogen and two nitrogen compressors are installed. For the installation more than 2 kilometers (1.25 miles) of hose-pipe is used. All lifting units are connected to a computer system that will precisely keep track of how much strain is put on each unit during the salvage operation. The system moreover is capable of simulating in advance all changes to the submarines center of gravity during both the loosening from the sea bottom and the actual raising process. During the journey of the Giant 4

to Kirkenes the engineers will extensively practice with the equipment. Just as on the AMT carrier, a home is built in the form of interconnected cargo containers for the 50-man crew.
Preparations for the diving work begin long before the reconstruction of the lifting pontoon.

A "getting to know each other" weekend is arranged in Aberdeen, Scotland – the home port of the Mayo – to let the experienced crew of divers get used to working with each other. They come from all over the world, Russia, Norway, Scotland, England, and even Australia. The professional divers world is

Several of the in total 26 nitrogen containers.

small, so for a number of them the meeting also feels like a reunion.

In the middle of July the Mayo is already underway to Kirkenes. Some time later the AMT carrier will leave from Rotterdam with the sawing installation. The two pontoons that will have to lift the Kursk with the Giant 4 when they will be moored into the dock in Murmansk, cannot be built in Western Europe, because the established shipyards there cannot meet the short delivery time. That is why this part of the contract is given to PO Sevmash in

Severodvinsk, only 2 days sailing time from Murmansk. In the record time of 9 weeks the Russian state company finishes building both colossi. To make this deadline, people are recruited from everywhere. Even already retired employees rally to the cause. They see it as an honor to be asked to participate in this endeavour. Jan van Seumeren comes up with the idea to name the pontoons after his wife and sister-in-law. And thus we have the names "Mar" and "Gon". Immediately both ladies are invited to perform the dockside christening ceremony.

The grippers are finished and anchored into the inner pipes on the Giant 4. Time is starting to press.

Between the acts, regular tests are conducted with the equipment that is already available. On various occasions, a delegation of Russians comes to Amsterdam to see for themselves how the specially developed equipment is performing. The Krylov Institute in St. Petersburg is also closely involved in this process. A great number of nautical tests are performed with scale models of the Giant 4 and the Kursk.

The pontoon Mar on the way from Severodvinsk to Murmansk.

Furthermore the grippers, the sawing system and the cutting equipment are extensively tested. These tests are crucially important; this is how it is verified if what was designed on the drawing board meets expectations in actual practice. These tests are not only a demand of the Russian government but also of the insurance company because every piece of equipment used has to be certified.

For months a great number of people is deployed to finish all preparations within the agreed upon time frame. Frans van Seumeren calls it "a match in which everybody only thinks of winning".

During this period he regularly dreams that his shoelaces snap just before an important soccer game!

For many, the operation means sacrificing their summer holiday vacation because the biggest time consuming parts of the work fall in the months of June, July and August. This high tech salvage operation is, and in the end remains, the work of people. Without this army of 2,000 dedicated laborers in various parts of the world, an operation like this, however cleverly thought through, could never be performed.

On August 28, 2001 the Giant 4 leaves Amsterdam and arrives at the sea locks of IJmuiden. Despite the late hour, hundreds of people are on the waterside cheering and waving flags in their hands to give the boat and their crew a warm send-off and fill the hearts of the salvagers with courage.

While the Giant 4 is on its way to Kirkenes, the Norwegian base of operation for the salvage operation, the divers on the Mayo are already busy with the first stages of the actual salvage operation. This takes place at longitude 69.37° N and latitude 37.19° E, at a depth of 110 meters, on the bottom of the ice-cold Barentsz Sea.

The stay-at-homes bid farewell to the salvagers.

04:32:28   THS 041 U   05/19/01

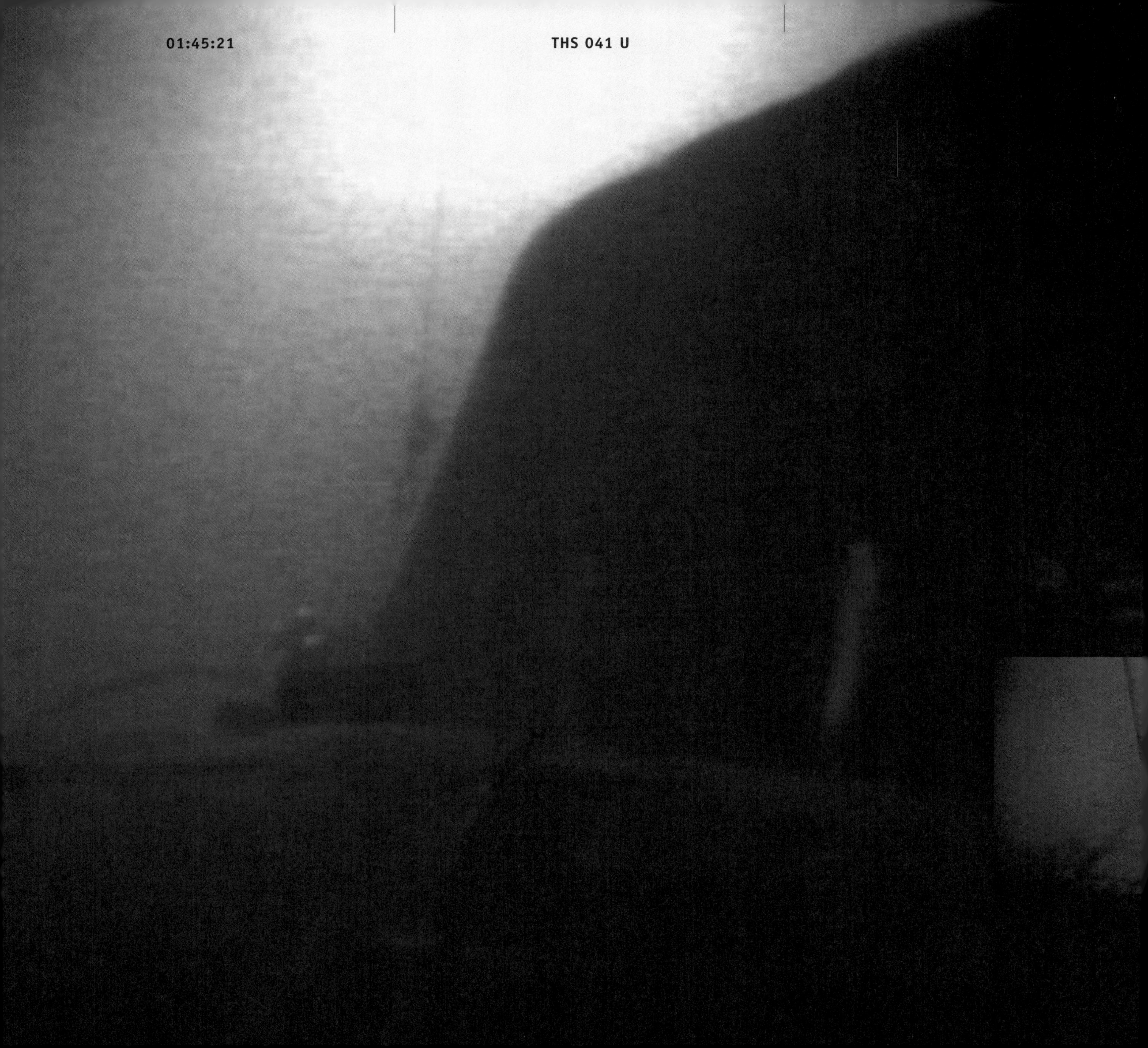
01:45:21
THS 041 U

Chapter 4 – The Salvage Operation

While engineers in Holland are still busy building up the Giant 4, the Mayo arrives on the Barentsz Sea and drops anchor above the site where the Kursk sank. The first real salvage activities begin.

A remote controlled robotic ROV camera is sent below to scope out the direct surroundings on the bottom and sends recorded pictures back up to the Mayo. On the diving vessel the crew catches its first glimpse of the sunken submarine. On one of the monitor screens, the damaged conning-tower looms. The realization hits the crew that it's not only a boat, but also a mass grave that contains the bodies of 106 Russian sailors. After a short period of reflection the first divers descend. The area around the site of the catastrophe first needs to be cleared, so there are no rocks, mud or pieces of the destroyed bow section in the way. The clearing is done with a so-called jet prop that uses water under high pressure to blow away objects that might obstruct the operation. Then begins the process of marking the spots on the hull where the holes need to be cut.

On the monitor diving super-intendant Wally Wallace sees one of the divers walk over the Kursk for the first time. The cutting of the holes into the hull is done under high pressure with a mixture of abrasive sand and water. First the outside skin is cut and then the inside skin. Regularly the divers lower themselves into a hole to clear away pipes, wires and other debris under the holes.

Later, there has to be space to easily lower the grippers into these holes. The divers are very experienced and used to salvaging bodies. Still they are relieved that they do not find any bodies in the places where they have to enter the submarine.

The AMT carrier with the sawing installation is still located in Kirkenes for last minute modifications to the sawing cable that will allow the crew to lengthen the maximum sawing time. That there is time for these modifications is a stroke of luck in the midst of the crisis. Because the cutting equipment at first doesn't cut well through the rubber skin of the Kursk, the divers cannot complete this stage of the salvage rapidly.

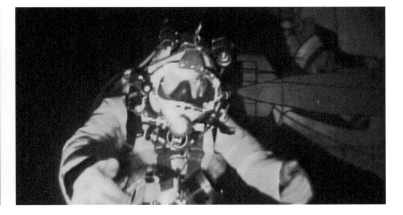

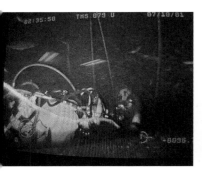

24 divers in groups of three work in 6-hour shifts. They are lowered to the Kursk in a diving bell, after which 2 of the 3 divers leave the bell. The third diver stays in the bell to monitor the work and to be able to immediately react in case of an emergency. The work is done at a depth of 110 meters (352 feet). The decompression process after a dive of 6-hours at this depth would take several days. To avoid losing precious time the divers there-fore stay in saturation, in a pressure tank on the Mayo, during the entire period at the Barentsz Sea. While diving, they use a mixture of oxygen and helium which gives their voices a Mickey Mouse-like sound.

For nearly a month they will continually be in the presence of one another in a tiny, elongated room where they have to eat, sleep, clean and relieve themselves. Through an air-lock their meals are handed to them by colleagues that monitor the environment in the pressure tank with meters, cameras and microphones, 24 hours a day. Although this simulates a 'Big Brother'- like situation, it is essential. They guard over the lives of the divers who fully depend on them all that time. The air lock also serves for garbage disposal. Each diver is provided with a small camera and a flash-light on his diving helmet and can communicate with his colleague diver on the sea bottom as well as with the diving superintendents on the Mayo. Through the little camera, they follow every under water movement from the surface. They can also instruct the divers exactly on which spots they have to cut. After 26 days the divers are replaced by a new team.

In the meantime the Giant 4 is on its way to Kirkenes. On the 30th of August the AMT carrier

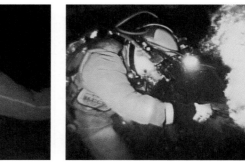

can finally leave the harbor of Kirkenes and sets course for the Mayo.

When the sawing pontoon has reached its destination, the divers are finally done with the holes. A new group is flown in by helicopter. Before the replaced divers can leave, they are screened with special measuring equipment for the level of radioactivity in their body. This happens with everybody and all of the equipment on the salvage location. Although various nuclear experts have extensively investigated the Kursk and have given the operation a green light, the safety of the people comes first. The measured radioactivity level during the entire salvage operation thankfully never exceeds the percentage that is normally measured in nature.

The new group of divers starts work by placing the suction anchors and the hydraulic cylinders that will drive the sawing cable. After that, the sawing cable is stretched over the Kursk on the place where the nose will be sawed off. On the 4th of September, the sawing installation is placed in operation. That seems to go successfully. After two and a quarter hours, already 25% of the nose has been sawed off.

Then a problem arises: the driving cable that connects the sawing cable on the left side with the cylinders snaps. The fracture is caused by friction with stones and other strange material on the bottom. They did not count on this. After thorough deliberation it is decided to place a kind of "mudguard" around the pulley that guides the driving cable, in fact an emergency solution. It seems to work, but this letdown costs a lot of time. The suction anchors sink during the sawing further and further into the sea bottom to maintain the ideal sawing angle of 20°. The suction anchor now has

The sawing pontoon and the Mayo on location.

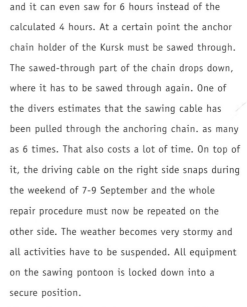

to be pulled out of the mud completely and the new driving cable has to be fitted in again. After one-and-a-half days the sawing process can begin again.

The emergency solution doesn't work optimally. The restlessness on board grows bigger. The pressure on the salvagers grows larger each day. When the driving cable breaks a second time, they are close to despair. Again the divers descend to repair the defect. The mudguard is reinforced and after the suction anchors have been pulled up yet again the men say a quick prayer. Unfortunately once again precious time has been lost. The sawing cable itself functions well,

and it can even saw for 6 hours instead of the calculated 4 hours. At a certain point the anchor chain holder of the Kursk must be sawed through. The sawed-through part of the chain drops down, where it has to be sawed through again. One of the divers estimates that the sawing cable has been pulled through the anchoring chain. as many as 6 times. That also costs a lot of time. On top of it, the driving cable on the right side snaps during the weekend of 7-9 September and the whole repair procedure must now be repeated on the other side. The weather becomes very stormy and all activities have to be suspended. All equipment on the sawing pontoon is locked down into a secure position.

The tension on board rises even more and fear starts to set in that the deadline of September the 15th cannot be met. The media throw oil onto the

The laying of a wreath on the bottom of the Barentsz Sea.

Smit International, responsible for contacts with the press. The ice-hockey arena in Murmansk is transformed into a press center. Why the deadline was missed is being explained to the assembled press corps. Mammoet wants to continue the salvage operation despite the weather becoming more and more unpredictable. The Russian as well as the Dutch experts reach the conclusion that the salvage of the Kursk is possible in the weeks that will follow. After the press conference, Frans flies back to Holland. Larissa stays in Murmansk.

On Friday, the 21st of September, the Giant 4 pulls anchor and sails out of Kirkenes Harbor on its way to the Kursk, which under normal weather conditions would take 2 days. The weather is not getting any better and the decision is made to pull up the grippers that were partially lowered the week before.

fire by suggesting that the salvage operation is going to fail. Tense days follow through the heavy weather and the crew can do nothing but wait for it to change.

That change comes thankfully and on the 11th of September they can continue. 2 Days later the bow is totally sawed off. The work for the sawing pontoon is finished and the crew returns to Kirkenes, where the Giant 4 lays waiting to enter the fray. A new crew is flown in and can begin with preparations and practicing the various previously worked out lifting scenarios. The grippers are already partially lowered in their tubes, which will save work on the Barentsz Sea. A part of the build-up

of the sawing pontoon, amongst which the cranes and the containers, is transferred onto the Giant 4. That was totally puzzled out during the preparations by Leo Versluis, so the salvagers can handle the available equipment as efficiently as possible and, in doing so, save costs.

On Wednesday, the 19th of September, Frans van Seumeren and his daughter Larissa leave for Murmansk. Larissa is, together with Lars Walder of

The lifting specialists on board the Giant 4 and the
divers at a depth of 110 meters work day and night.

As the weather becomes even worse and the weather forecasters predict waves of 4-6 meters (15-20 feet), Captain Piet Sinke turns the pontoon around to seek shelter behind a small island. Almost immediately there is radio contact with the announcement "you're sailing the wrong way!" This is proof that the operation is being closely monitored by the principal. Finally, the Giant 4 arrives on the 26th of September at its destination and is welcomed by the Mayo and the Cruiser Peter the Great, owing that name because it is the largest ship of the entire Russian Fleet. However, the weather is becoming worse and worse.

In the meantime, the divers are doing everything in their power with specially developed equipment to remove all the still present material around the holes of the inside skin to make sure that the grippers can be easily installed later on. This is also not exactly a cakewalk. And again the salvage operation is slowed. The journalists start to stir again.

Larissa and Lars have a full-time job explaining what is going on and trying to silence rumors before they start such as "the Kursk is not being salvaged this year". On the contrary, the entire crew is still convinced the salvage can be successfully completed, before the Barentsz Sea turns into a permanent Hell. When all the holes are finally cleaned the most important stage of the project, the lifting operation, can begin.

It takes an entire day to anchor the Giant 4 securely above the wreckage of the Kursk. First, with the help of an ROV underwater robot, gripper guides are installed on the holes of the inside skin.

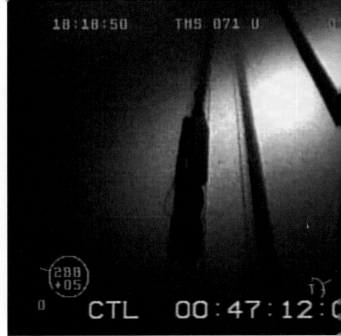

The gripper guides have the shape of a ring and make sure that the grippers can be easily guided inside through the hole.

In order to guide a gripper accurately to the sea bottom and get it exactly above the hole, the next step is to lower 4 so-called re-entry lines and attach them to the ring, that has been placed on the gripper guide.

Meanwhile on board the Giant 4, the lifting specialists bring the containers with liquid nitrogen to their proper pressure. And then the team waits for a quieter sea to begin installing the grippers. When the weather improves, the divers again go down in 6-hour cycles. As a test, the lifting specialists lower the first four rings and re-entry lines. The divers have no trouble with assembling them. Within an hour the rings and the lines are connected 110 meters (352 feet) beneath the lifting pontoon. On board they now know for sure that the attaching system works.

Unfortunately another storm arises, which means that the grippers still cannot be lowered. On the 1st of October the first 2 grippers are installed. It is not going very quickly because every gripper is unique and has to be lowered into the Kursk at a certain angle; 2 a day however, is way too slow. In total 26 grippers have to go in. The media strike again giving negative messages and once more both press representatives head onto the barricades. In Holland, Frans van Seumeren can't stand it any

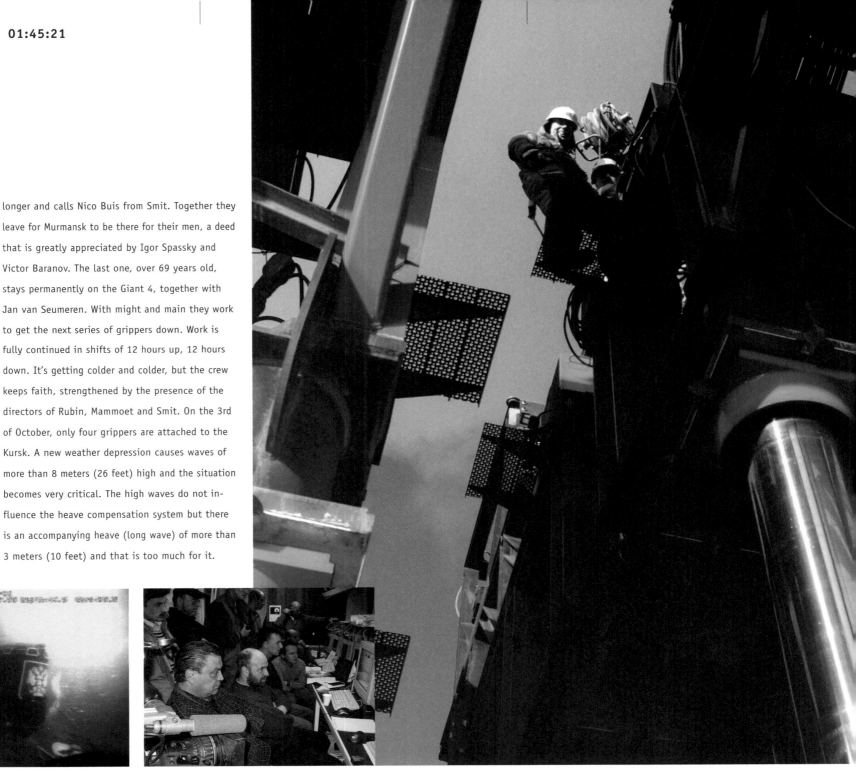

5.3M

longer and calls Nico Buis from Smit. Together they leave for Murmansk to be there for their men, a deed that is greatly appreciated by Igor Spassky and Victor Baranov. The last one, over 69 years old, stays permanently on the Giant 4, together with Jan van Seumeren. With might and main they work to get the next series of grippers down. Work is fully continued in shifts of 12 hours up, 12 hours down. It's getting colder and colder, but the crew keeps faith, strengthened by the presence of the directors of Rubin, Mammoet and Smit. On the 3rd of October, only four grippers are attached to the Kursk. A new weather depression causes waves of more than 8 meters (26 feet) high and the situation becomes very critical. The high waves do not in-fluence the heave compensation system but there is an accompanying heave (long wave) of more than 3 meters (10 feet) and that is too much for it.

Jan van Seumeren can do nothing more than pick one of the previously thought-out emergency scenarios off-the-shelf.

Heave compensation is put to silence and the cables with which the 4 grippers are attached, are slackened with 10 meters. In no case the crew can be exposed to too great a risk. Meanwhile, Frans van Seumeren stays with Nico Buis, Igor Spassky and Mikhail Barskov on the Mayo and they maintain contact with the Giant 4 through satellite telephone. The heavy storm heaves both ships violently up and down.

After 2 days it looks like the wind is subsiding and they can continue to lower the grippers. Then there is the announcement that a new storm is on its way, even more furious than the previous one. Now that the Kursk is already attached to the Giant 4 on 4 points, there is no turning back. It's now or never. There is a real chance that the Giant 4 will be beaten off of its anchors. If that happens then the salvage attempt is over. Then the salvagers will have no other option left: they will have to cut the lines. Everybody waits stoically. Nobody can do anything.

On the Mayo tension also rises, but for a totally different reason. Nico Buis tells Frans van Seumeren that he is starting to doubt if the salvage can still be done, considering the past delays, the weather problems and the financial consequences that come with it. He feels like quitting and going home. Contractually, Mammoet could stop because there is a clause in the salvage contract which says bad weather can be a reason to suspend the operation: this is left to the judgement of Mammoet alone. Van Seumeren calls in Spassky and Barskov and the four of them retreat for a crisis consultation. The two Russians leave no doubt that they want the salvage success-fully completed. They do not like it at all that Nico Buis is putting on pressure to stop the operation. Taunted they look Frans van Seumeren in the eye, who remembers very well what he has promised them not even 4 months ago. He thinks a moment and nods his head. "We have to carry on, we will get him out", he says. Spassky looks at him intensely for 10 seconds and then nods slowly, immediately followed by Barskov. Buis in the end finally goes along with the decision; everybody takes a deep breath. The salvage operation enters its most critical stage.

A day later the most voilent storm during the entire operation dies down. A huge surge of relief is felt by everyone aboard.

The crew can continue. They start lowering and assembling the grippers. The tempo rises and two days later 16 pieces are installed. The last 10 are lowered in record time and the weather holds. The decision of Frans van Seumeren and his team seems to be a good one. When a lifting capacity of 150 tons is set on all 26 lifting points, the crew feels a little movement on board the Giant 4, an indication that the Kursk is not as solidly stuck in the mud as had been expected. On the night of 7-8 October, the lifting platforms can be put fully into operation and the raising of the Kursk begins. After a couple of hours the Giant 4 sinks a tiny bit further into the sea. Air bubbles are seen on the surface. The Kursk is loose! An enormous wave of relief washes over the crew. The carefully thought-out system works in reality. When the Kursk is approximately 15 meters (about 50 feet) above the bottom of the sea, Piet Sinke lifts the anchor and turns the Giant 4 into the wind. Very slowly the lifting pontoon is pulled forward by tugboats, while lifting continues. Wessel Helmens, Victor Baranov, Igor Ovdienko,

Baranov cuts the cake.

Jan Kleijn and the others present in the control room watch mesmerized at the computer screens and adjust the pulling power per lifting point when necessary.

10 Hours later they feel the Kursk touch the Giant 4. Two gigantic masses bump against each other a couple of times before the Kursk sits tightly against the saddles. The relief is gigantic and there is time for a brief celebration. The cook on board has specially baked a cake for the occasion. The crew though cannot enjoy it for long, because Murmansk is not yet in sight and the wind is rising again. On Wednesday the 10th of October, the Giant 4 with underneath it the Kursk arrives at the floating dock in the harbor of Roslyakova, a stone's throw distance from Murmansk. The colossal

combination of 24.000 ton (53.5 million pounds) is moored in the bay, under the loud horn tooting of a flotilla of Russian ships.
The next day the last part of the operation has to begin. The crew gets to choose between being relieved or staying. A part of the crew goes home, dead-tired, a part also decides to stay for the docking. The Press Center though is almost empty. The eyes of the news world are directed on the threatened war in Afghanistan, an after-effect of the catastrophe on the 11th of September, the day the twin towers of the WTC in New York collapsed.

Darkness falls and it starts to snow. The pontoons Mar and Gon are laying in the dark, waiting for their task that will commence the next day.

Tired but satisfied, the crew of the
Giant 4 enjoys a hot cup of coffee.

Chapter 5 – The Homecoming

Now that the Kursk is in Russian waters again, the Russian Navy wants to take over control. A couple of tugboats are guided into the bay and two admirals come aboard the Giant 4. This causes a lot of tension, because until that moment the command was in the hands of Jan van Seumeren and that is a "civil command". The crew is not used to military authority, therefore communication does not flow subtly. The Russians see the mooring of the Kursk into dry-dock as a task of honor while Mammoet wants to finish the operation – the last phase of the assignment. There are some heavy discussions. Finally Jan van Seumeren persuades the Russians

not to interfere with the operational management and the admirals leave the Giant 4. However, there is a Russian camera crew that comes aboard to record all events. These are broadcasted every evening on Russian television.

It is not easy for the Russian military to watch. The civilian crew works in an apparently undisciplined manner, walks through one another on the pontoon and it doesn't at all resemble a tight military approach. This is however, merely an appearance. Because they are so well tuned-in to each other after their long stay in Kirkenes and on the Barentsz Sea, one word or a gesture is often sufficient to make clear to each other what needs to happen.

The tugboats bring the pontoons Mar and Gon close to the Giant 4/Kursk combination. Winter has definitely made his entrance. It starts to snow and blow, the temperature falls to -8°C (17.6° F). All kinds of equipment begin to freeze on-deck and part of the overly tired crew becomes ill and shows flu symptoms. On top of that, after inspection, a couple of flaps of outside skin from the nose of the Kursk are in the way. Those have to be cut-off.

And if that is not enough, problems occur with the pontoons. To get them to both slide under the combination, the Mar and Gon have to be half sunk letting water run into them. After that they are placed under the Giant 4 with the aid of tugboats, air can be pumped into them which will cause the combination to rise.

The Gon gets the first turn. What should be correct in theory, does not work in reality and with the rushing in of water, the pontoon capsizes. There are problems with its stability. A solution is found by welding extra floats onto the pontoons. The Mar is also not showing her best side and manifests the same defect. Again Russian divers go into the water. Only on the 19th of October the stability problems are overcome. The Mar and Gon are attached to both sides under the Giant 4/Kursk and the pumping can begin. To be towed into the dock the 24,000 ton heavy (24 million kilos!) (53 million pounds!) Giant 4/Kursk combination has to rise about 7 meters.

Again a problem occurs: after a day of pumping, the desired height has not been reached.

Measuring radioactivity during docking.

The team decides to remove finished materials from the Giant 4 to reduce the weight of the combination. After some 220 tons (220,000 kilos) (almost 500,000 pound) are removed and 600 tons (1.2 million pounds) of ballast water pumped away, the height needed is reached.

These unforeseen problems, as it happens, add an 8-day delay, but on October 21st all is completed. 12 Russian tugboats, a number of Navy officers and 50 sailors are sent in to pull the combination into the

dock. Around midnight, The Kursk sits in her dry-dock. The following day the 26 grippers are loosened and removed. Arjan Braspenning, a crew member from Mammoet, reverently in memory of the deceased crewmembers, closes a hatch that was still open.

On October 23rd, at 9:28 a.m. Dutch time the moment is there: mission completed!

A minute of silence follows. Together with Victor Baranov, Piet Sinke drops a wreath into the water.

The crew watches, caps in hand. On the shore the Russian Navy forms a guard of honor for their 106 country-men that finally return to shore. The Giant 4 can now leave the dry-dock.

After 5 months of extraordinarily hard work, the salvage project received from the Russian Government on the 18th of May is successfully completed.

During the following days the Mar and Gon are towed out from under the Giant 4 and on the 29th

of October the return trip of the Giant to Holland begins. The most extensive and innovative lifting operation in the history of Mammoet becomes an historic event. The major part of the crew returns home by airplane and receives an hero's welcome at Schiphol Airport.

The Russian people's celebration of the homecoming of the Kursk is partly overshadowed by grief. The definitive determination of the disasters cause and the raising of the bodies is followed by a memorial worship service at the St. Nicholas Church in St. Petersburg which pulls deep traces of grief. The late Lieutenant Captain Dmitri Romanovich Koleshnikov, on whose body a last letter to his wife was found, becomes an icon of the tragedy.

The raising creates an unbreakable bond of friendship between Mammoet and Rubin. More than one year after the homecoming of the Kursk, Frans and Jan van Seumeren, together with several of their employees receive the Order of Friendship from the Russian Ambassador in the Netherlands. This order, created in 1994 by then President Yeltsin, is granted to people who substantially contribute to the strengthening of friendship and international partnership in the areas of knowledge, culture, economics and peace.

The "raising" file is closed, but the "friendship" file remains open permanently.

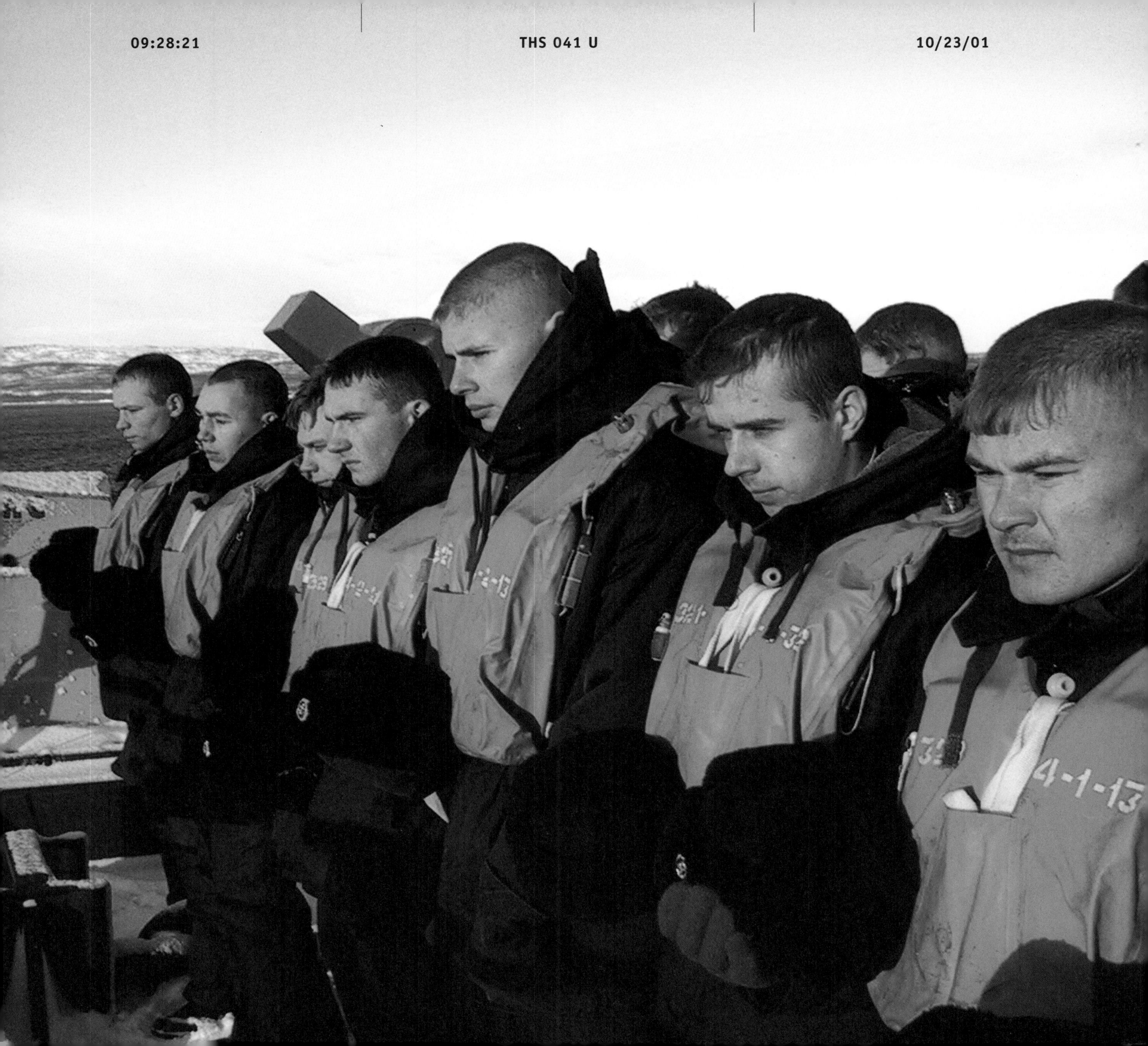
09:28:21
THS 041 U
10/23/01
4-1-13

Part 2 - **Personal Impressions**

Frans van Seumeren

Name Frans van Seumeren

Age 53

Function President & CEO Mammoet

Role in the Project Overall responsibility

Number of service years to Mammoet 34

When I heard from the media that the Kursk had sunk, I immediately thought: this is a job for us. A real "lifting job", but with special complications. Normally at a salvage, there is a lot of rough and violent pulling and picking, but here that was not possible because there was an enormous nuclear risk. In the beginning of October, I called Slava Zakharov the director of our branch in Moscow and asked him to find out on whose door we needed to knock to submit a proposal. In the meantime we went on with drawing and making plans.

In January Slava called back and announced that he had managed to make an appointment with Igor Spassky, general director of Rubin, the Russian company that designed and built the Kursk. Rubin performed also as principal in the name of the Russian government. Our company, by the way, was already known in Russia because we have lifted the roof of the Olympic Stadium in Moscow with strandjacks in the past.

At Rubin we were received with a lot of respect and I presented drawings and sketches to show how we wanted to basically approach it. Spassky was very interested in the use of our tested strandjacks, but let it be known that we were too late. They were already in long-standing negotiations with the consortium of Smit, Heerema and Halliburton and they wanted to proceed with those parties. If I wanted to join, I had to direct myself to them.

In the background the Kursk Foundation also played a role. It tried to let a couple of Western European companies work together with Russia and salvage the Kursk on a basis of shared cost risk, because this was desirable from both a humanitarian and environmental view. The Kursk Foundation had already decided to do business with the consortium and I knew that it was almost impossible to break into that closed circle. So I went home but I was not deeply disappointed. At Mammoet it was not yet widely known that we were trying to get this assignment.

And then I didn't hear anything anymore. Until in early April, 2001, more than 3 months later, I was called by Slava. He had spoken with Spassky and they asked me to come to St. Petersburg secretly right away. It turned out that some difficulties had arisen with the consortium and the promised financing wasn't raised. I also heard that the consortium let it be known that the salvage could not be completed in 2001. That was especially unpleasant for Rubin, because President Putin had promised the Russian people that the bodies of the crew would be salvaged that year.

I realized that the time plan was very short, because there is such bad weather in the Barentsz Sea in September that a salvage operation would be very difficult to mount. Including the negotiations to come, we would have barely 5 months to get the whole job done. I agreed with Spassky that I would go back to Holland to confer with my brother Jan and would let them know within 5 days if we were going to do the job or not. Well, in short, the answer was YES and then everything was accelerated enormously. We traveled with a technical team to Rubin to walk them through the whole process while in Holland I gave the assignment to Leo Versluis to go and claim the production capacity we would need with sub-contractors. Imagine, in 4 months time about 5,000 ton (5 million kilos) of steel would be formed into equipment that was needed for the salvage operation. I was also convinced it would be a good thing to involve Smit. Mammoet has experience at sea, but primarily with tugging objects above the water so we needed a good maritime partner.

And while our people in Holland were already very busy with the preparations, Jan, Wessel and Klaas sat in negotiations with the technical people of Rubin about the definitive approach. They were, by the way, very impressed with the knowledge of their Russian technical colleagues, that only weren't acquainted with the heave compensation system. I had to solve some tricky points with Spassky that Leo had already prepared because I was, at that moment, in Greece. It concentrated on the law the contract would be under, the insurance risk, the timeline and the payment schedule. When we finally signed the contract on the 18th of May 2001, we had not totally solved it but found a solution in a side letter. We were assisted by an English lawyer. She did a fantastic job and crafted the side letter into a contract a week later.

"Looking back I think the project was blessed because no one was wounded and everybody working on the salvage came home safely."

During the preparations Spassky and I limited ourselves to the signing of the milestone documents and spoke with each other regularly during the test stages of the equipment, because Rubin wanted everything to be tested in advance. My brother Jan was the 1st responsible boss of the project during the salvage operation and stayed all that time on the Giant 4. When the weather became very bad on the Barentsz Sea in September, I had to go there. I couldn't stay at home any longer. The rate at which the grippers were being lowered, would mean that we could only start lifting in November. That was unacceptable. Nico Buis wanted to quit, watching the financial risks become bigger and bigger... as the delays stacked further up. I wanted to prevent that. Also I had to convince Spassky that the submarines head was completely sawed off because that was a milestone for one of the payments. Spassky at first did not want to believe me, but finally changed his mind and signed the approval notice. In fairness, looking back, I have to say that he nevertheless was right. Measurements revealed that a tiny piece of the head was still attached to the hull. When we started lifting the head thankfully it broke off almost immediately. I never doubted that we could bring the salvage to a happy end, but at that moment, I had a very difficult time.

On the way to Murmansk we passed a very tiny church in the middle of nowhere. I am not a religious man, but I felt the need to go inside. In that place I found a kind of power and peace and looking back I think this project was blessed because no one was wounded and everybody working on the salvage came home safely. Next to that we have always realized ourselves that were not only busy with a boat but also with the salvage of the bodies of 106 fellow human beings.

Left: Frans van Seumeren with vice-admirals Motzak and Barskov from the Russian navy.

Right: Frans van Seumeren with Igor Spassky (left) and Nico Buis (right).

Jan van Seumeren

Name Jan van Seumeren

Age 52

Funtion Technical Advisor, Mammoet

Role in the Project Technical and operational end responsibility

Number of service years to Mammoet 34

When the Kursk sank and my brother Frans said that could mean a very nice lifting job for Mammoet, I immediately started thinking. In my favorite pub, with a beer on the side, I made the first rough drawings of the final system that salvaged the Kursk on the back of a beer coaster. The beer coaster is now placed in the Mammoet archives.

In the beginning we were closed out of the bidding process, but when we came back in the race in April 2001, I took the beer coaster out of the cupboard. Within 5 days we decided together that we would present a proposal to Rubin to salvage the Kursk in that same year. Together with Wessel Helmens and Klaas Lamphen, I traveled down to St. Petersburg. The conferences with the engineers of Rubin began and I understood fairly quickly that they had already considered our plans themselves. What was new to them, were the grippers in combination with the computer operated heave compensation system that we thought was necessary to neutralize the swell of the waves in the Barentsz Sea.

We had an enormous amount of help from the Russian translator and engineer, Anna Skorokhodova, the right hand of director Spassky. After a couple of days we noticed that the Russians did want to give us information but were not used to it. After all it was a military secret. However, we needed to know it for technical reasons. At one point I literally said, "help us because we don't know how to proceed further". That was a breakthrough point in the discussions. From that moment on a mutual respect developed that Mammoet and Rubin had to do it together. Anna played a very important role in the growing of this understanding. I do not want to leave that unmentioned. We entered a routine of talks, re-adjusting the plans, faxing to De Meern, new drawings immediately turned around to St. Petersburg and that for 3 days at a stretch. What we imagined and created in the morning was off the drawing table in Holland and back in Russia the same afternoon. Technical people, from wherever in the world they come,

The reception by Putin in the Kremlin (Jan van Seumeren stands 2nd from left).

can understand each other very quickly with a drawing: no words needed. Slava Zakharov, our director in Russia, also did a tremendous job in letting the two cultures understand each other better.

Sometimes it was very intimidating. We were there with the 3 of us, sitting at a very wide table, opposite us the enormous group of 25 Russian engineers, that with every adjustment went to an internal consultation and deliberation again. In the end we reached a point where we wanted a letter of intent before we would put all of our knowledge on the table and then run the risk that there would be no signed contract. That is why I said to Spassky that I wanted a signed document. Mountains had to be moved but in the end we went home with a signed letter of intent. In the following months, Frans worked that out into a final contract and we could begin the final preparations.

During the preparations the Russians came to Holland very often because they wanted to test everything and what could not be tested in Holland had to go to Russia. The Krylov Institute in St. Petersburg for example tested the lifting power of the grippers to ensure they could easily withstand two times the required strength. They finally stopped testing because the draw bench started to make suspicious creaking noises!

In this stage the confidence between the Russian and Dutch engineers grew and that was an important basis for the success of the enterprise. I developed a deep bond with Baranov, the designer of the Kursk and in the end we led the whole operation on board the Giant 4 working shoulder-to-shoulder, shared the critical moments on the

"With a beer on the side, on the back of a beer coaster, I made the first rough drawings of the system that finally salvaged the Kursk."

Barentsz Sea and the emotional moments when the Kursk came loose, when we showed respect to the deceased whilst back in the port. I can say that in Baranov I have found a friend for life.

The gratitude that we were allowed to receive from the Russians involved but later in Holland as well, touched me deeply and made me realize that probably only once in your life you may undertake such an honor-filled assignment.

Jan van Seumeren with right hand Klaas Lamphen.

Leo Versluis

Name Leo Versluis

Age 51

Function Director Tendering

Role in the Project Overall project coordinator,
responsible for planning and managing the project managers.
Primary contact person for Rubin

Number of service years to Mammoet 28

In April 2001, Frans van Seumeren was asked to come to St. Petersburg because Smit/Heerema/Halliburton had dropped out. He said that I had to become project manager and gave me an explanation of the project. At first I approached it rather skeptically and thought it was not possible to do the job in the mentioned time frame. But after talking with Jan van Seumeren, Klaas Lamphen and Wessel Helmens, I slowly became more enthusiastic. They had prepared a lot of technical designs and there were already contacts with sub-contractors. Shortly after I had had the briefing, the contracts were signed and I could start. The financial planning also was my task, so I had to know the content of the contracts to the letter. The top-end of the total amount was more or less known and I of course needed that in the negotiations with the subcontractors.

For me a time started in which I had to out-source millions of dollars of work in a couple of weeks. With this I had a lot of help from Jan Kleijn. Picture this: everything was drafted in English and then translated into Russian. For the finance and the insurance I went to Russia together with the people from AON and ABN-AMRO. After 2 days of negotiation we had a workable concept agreement over the payments, insurance and likewise. There were still some tricky points left that Frans van Seumeren solved later.

When the contract was signed on the 18th of May, I was in Holland already very busily outsourcing work. This required more than 16 million dollars and I found it a very special experience that I could "spend" so much money in just a couple of weeks.

A week later I had to go back to Russia for a short period of time with a group of technical people to agree on all kinds of affairs like: the lifting power, the weather conditions, ships on location, medical arrangements in case someone got injured, helicopters, accommodations on the worksite, availability of Russian divers and so on. When this was all agreed upon, the financial planning had to be assembled. We used milestones for that. The work was accurately defined and divided into 16 stages. Each stage was separately estimated and paid. For example: the moment the divers depart from Aberdeen, the departure of the Giant 4 from Amsterdam, the cutting of the holes in the Kursk, the docking, and so on. As soon as a stage was completed, documents had to be signed by 5 people: the gentlemen Spassky and Baranov for Rubin, Admiral Barskov for the Russian Navy and Frans van Seumeren and myself for Mammoet. After the signing the money was transferred. At the start of the project the total amount was put in a bank account in Utrecht.

The financial planning and payment schedule were set up in a way that we would still get break-even if we couldn't do the actual lifting. Mammoet was contractually bound to decide, for safety reasons, whether the raising could begin on the Barentsz Sea or had to be terminated because of bad weather conditions. Should we be unable to execute the hoisting and docking, in any case the preparation costs were covered. We had a lot of extremely bad weather, but luckily the entire operation was successfully completed, humanitarianly and technically, as well as financially.

"When the contract was signed on the 18th of May, I was in Holland already very busily outsourcing work. This required more than 16 million dollars and I found it a very special experience that I could 'spend' so much money in just a couple of weeks."

Jan Kleijn

Name Jan Kleijn

Age 35

Function Director Operations/Engineering

Role in the Project At the preparation: responsible for building
all new steel constructions and their installation on the Giant 4.
At the salvage: responsible for the strandjack system.

Number of service years to Mammoet 5

*"Everybody said something
like, 'this is Hollands Glory'
and they would gladly
co-operate with that."*

In April, 2001 Jan van Seumeren asked me to gather information about available capacity from our regular suppliers.
There was no contract signed as yet with Rubin and I had to move cautiously and keep my requests a bit vague for
the total desired production capacity. We needed more than 20 strandjacks for the raising and I only had 8 in-house.
If you then place an order for 12, people start thinking "Why do you need such a large number?" I think that by
placing these orders before the contract, Mammoets plan leaked out before its' time, but there was not much we
could do about it, because we had such short preparation time. I had to deal with suppliers throughout the whole
country of Holland, from Roermond to IJmuiden. The reactions were all very positive. Everybody said something
like, "this is Hollands Glory" and they would gladly co-operate with that. All of Mammoets close relationships
were immediately willing to deliver the extra effort, holidays were cancelled and everybody was motivated to work
together on the project. I also had to deal with a couple of suppliers with whom we had never worked before.
I have nothing but praise for them by the way. But I had to come to them with very awkward questions about
their inventory and production times and I could not exactly tell them how much I needed of certain materials,
when it had to be delivered and so on - not only time, but also the quality level in relation to a realistic price
was an important factor.

Normally we work according to a fixed concept: basic engineering, detailed engineering and then product
development. However, that couldn't fly now, because during the preparations we engineered, built, re-engineered
and rebuilt. And we got more and more information from the Russians as they understood how we wanted to handle
the project. They also demanded a lifting capacity that was 2 times greater than what we calculated.

All the equipment and tools that we built also had to be certified by Lloyds for insurance reasons. The building up of the Giant 4 was an enormous operation. Sometimes it was just like Disneyland in Amsterdam on the shipyard. When we went through the locks at IJmuiden on our way to Kirkenes, there was an enormous crowd of people that came to watch us with their children. They stood there applauding and while we hadn't yet done a thing, the 'Hollands Glory' feeling could already be strongly felt. On our way to Norway we made all kinds of adjustments to the equipment. That was also planned so we could use the weeks at sea efficiently.

The preparation stage was very strenuous for everybody. Getting everything ready and on board was an enormous accomplishment. But I keep seeing see this project in two stages, preparation and lifting.

The media attention for the project was weakened in the second stage by the terrible disaster in America on September 11th. It completely passed me by on that moment because I was totally focused on the salvage operation and that was the case for all our colleagues too.

"4 Months of preparation against 15 hours of lifting!"

When the Kursk stands on the dry-dock blocks, the water is pumped out, after which the salvagers take their first steps on the conning-tower of the Kursk.

Your awareness of the time passing becomes totally lost. To work under pressure like that for weeks you really get to know your colleagues very well. When the Kursk hung under the Giant 4, I felt an enormous feeling of relief. The second stage successfully passed. If you then look at the time spent it is very strange. 4 Months of preparation against 15 hours of lifting!

The loosening of the Kursk from the ocean floor is best compared with the movement of the pendulum of a very heavy clock. It was a very exciting moment, but when the Kursk touched the Giant 4 that was even more exciting because then you have two very big masses together, enormous powers that have to match. You heard the saddles squeak and bump.

Then we went on our way to Murmansk, to the dock. We thought we would be welcomed as heroes but we still had to go through Customs and Immigration control as normal. We were helped with the docking by the Russians. They felt it was their project and so that is how it was explained to the press. Anyhow, most of us became ill during the docking. Once the tension is broken, more often than not, something like that happens.

The first time I walked on the deck of the Kursk and finally saw what it was that we lifted it was very difficult to look at the tower with the broken windows. You know you don't dare look inside. The human aspect of this whole operation came crushing down and that stays with you.

Luckily I also have very beautiful memories of the operation. I saw the Northern Lights for the first time in my life and once a school of porpoises swam by. At night, when I couldn't sleep during the storms on the Barentsz Sea, I went outside and felt the elements all around me.

Piet Sinke

Name Piet Sinke

Age 44

Function Marine Operations Manager

Role in the Project Captain of the Giant 4

Number of service years to Smit 26

At the moment Mammoet won the assignment for the salvage of the Kursk, I was on a job in Greece. After coming home I was called by Hans van Rooij (a director of Smit International). I had to come immediately to the crisis center in De Meern where I was told what we were going to do. Now we are reasonably experienced in special, tough jobs: the building of the second Benelux tunnel, a bridge in Patras and a tunnel in Singapore. But the Kursk was something completely different.

After the briefing in De Meern, we started the maritime preparations right away. The most important thing was to choose a base of operation that was the best for maritime technical purposes. That is why we chose Kirkenes; we could import all equipment through Norway instead of Russia, which surely would have caused administrative difficulties. In Kirkenes we organized a meeting with Customs, Immigration, the hospital and various important people from the shipyard and harbor. At the rescue coordination center in Norway we also arranged a stand-by helicopter for emergencies.

The Kursk lay in international waters and while a helicopter could reach the Giant from Norwegian soil, it would not have enough fuel to return. That is why a Norwegian spy ship, the Marjata was asked to stay in contact reach.

Back in Holland a lot of time went into writing all of the procedures and the search for a suitable pontoon for the sawing unit that would be used to remove the nose of the Kursk. We found an English one in Vlissingen, which was then brought to Rotterdam and rebuilt by Verolme IJsselmonde.

"We sailed through the middle of a military exercise area for the Russian Navy and once had to seek shelter from a storm behind a little island, that's how bad it was."

Piet Sinke asks the crew to take off

their hats for a moment of silence.

We also had to arrange a tugboat for the sawing barge that could bring her to the location above the Kursk and winches for hoisting the anchors. Besides all this, there were daily consultations with the engineers at Mammoet.

Once the Giant 4 lay in Kirkenes, we had to wait for suitable weather to sail into the Barentsz Sea. We sailed through the middle of a military exercise area for the Russian Navy and once had to seek shelter from a storm behind a little island, that's how bad it was. Without noticing, we got in the middle of a military exercise and I suddenly saw all kinds of periscopes come above water and we were immediately hailed over the radio and told to leave. Once above the Kursk, we had to drop anchor. That process is done with very sensitive audio equipment, because it is reasonably complicated to get exactly above it because the holes and the lifting units had to precisely lay opposite each other, with about 100 meters (330 feet) of seawater in between them.

We couldn't let all the gripper be lowered continuously; the weather-conditions were fluctuating too much. On a certain moment the sea became so high, that we had to make a decision if we would continue or not. By loosening the cables of the lifting units that were already attached to the Kursk, we could ride out the storm. We had to bob around topside for 5 days until the weather changed for the better. Then the attachment of the grippers went pretty quickly and we could start lifting. Until the Kursk was loosened from the sea bottom, you could only see that on the vessel (the Giant 4) and on the computer program. When the Kursk hung about 15 meters (almost 50 feet) above the bottom of the sea, we could pull her over the sawn off bow section and turn the Giant 4 well into the wind. 10 hours later she was tightly against the saddles and we pointed the stern towards Murmansk to dock the Kursk.

Personally, I found the docking the most critical part because we were too heavy for the dry-dock. After cutting, sliding and pulling loose equipment we were 220 tons lighter and could finally go into the dry-dock.

But the most touching moment for me was the wreath laying ceremony together with the Russians during the departure of the dry-dock.

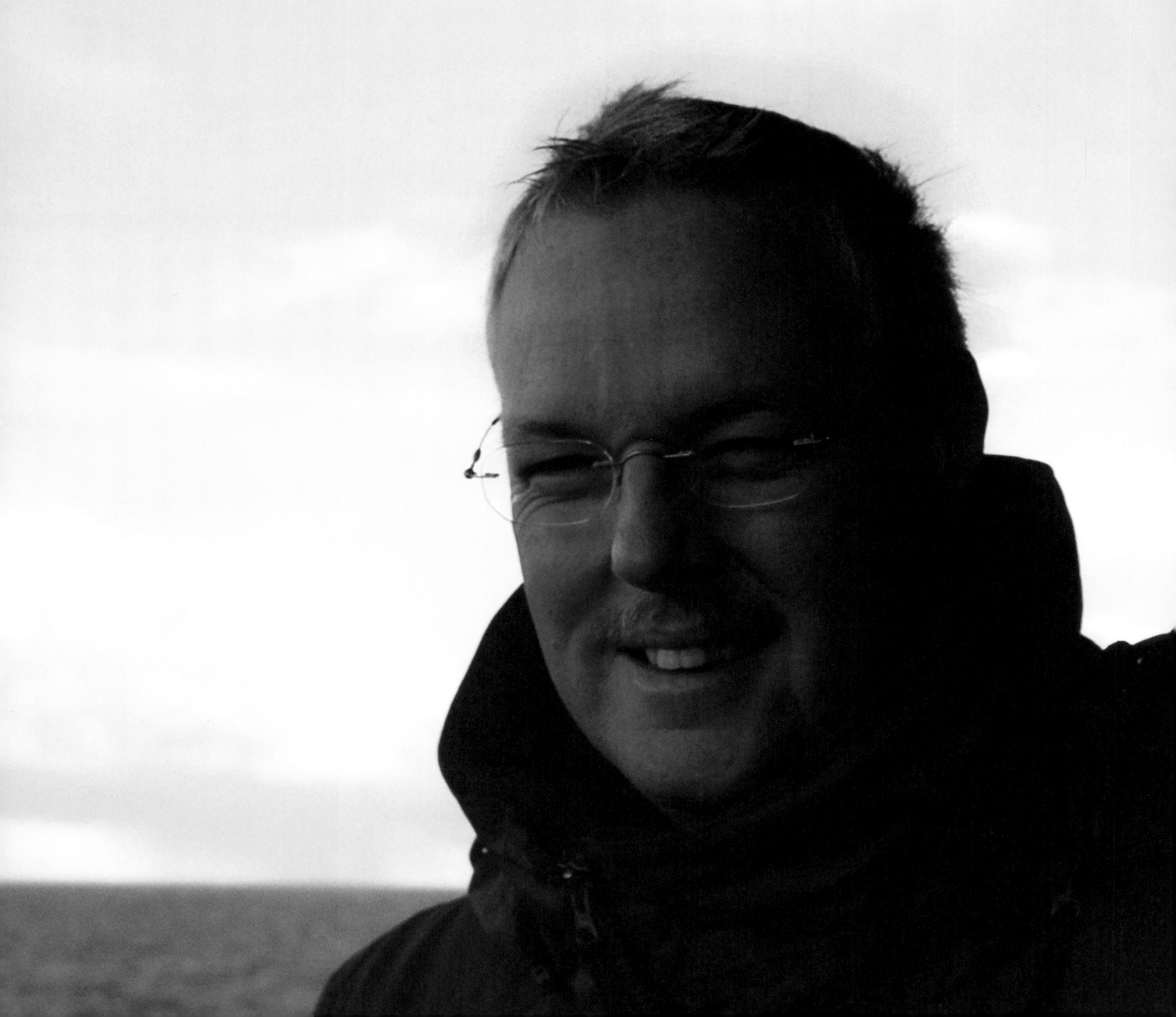

Wessel Helmens

Name Wessel Helmens

Age 45

Function Engineering Manager

Role in the Project 1st phase – preparations; responsible for all engineering;

2nd phase – salvage operation; primary contactperson for the Russian engineers

on board the Giant 4

Number of service years to Mammoet 7

For me, the project really started the moment Jan van Seumeren, Klaas Lamphen and I boarded the airplane to St. Petersburg. Frans van Seumeren let Rubin know we were willing to perform the salvage job. During the flight we made some adjustments to the drafts and drawings. The next morning we were received at Rubin. Anyways, the hotel where we stayed was a part of the same complex. It was an old building, with enormous doors. We were guided to the big hall where the meetings would take place. It was totally refurbished especially for the project. There was a distinct atmosphere in the air and I had the feeling we were constantly being watched. At the first presentation 25 people were present. These were people that were used to designing a new submarine over a period of ten years. Now they had to think of something in only a couple of months to salvage one. On 6 double-wide sheets of paper, we showed them how we wanted to perform the salvage operation. We pretty quickly noticed that our Russian colleagues had already invested 6 months of thinking into the salvage method. So they had very clearly worked out that the Kursk had to be lifted through lifting points attached to the hull), while at Mammoet we had thought at first using a system with bands underneath the submarine. The head had to be sawed off. That was clear, only we didn't yet know how. In the beginning, the Russians were not so forthcoming with information but when after 2 days Jan made clear that he really could not do this without their help, the ice quickly thawed. The feeling that we were being watched made space for a feeling of united cooperation. I too became very impressed with the expertise of the Russian engineers. They knew very well the best way to perform the salvage. They only weren't as far along concerning the heave compensation system, the strandjacks and the sawing off of the nose. After 3 days of meetings, translating, meetings, faxing to Holland and back to St. Petersburg with adjusted drawings, Jan said to Spassky (Director of Rubin): "Now I want a 'letter of intent', because we have reached an agreement in

"These were people that were used to designing a new submarine over a period of ten years. Now they had to think of something in only a couple of months to salvage one."

Wessel Helmens and colleagues prepare themselves for the lifting operation by practicing various scenarios with the help of a simulation program.

principle and I am not going to explain any further details without a signed document". That was very un-Russian and mountains had to be moved to get that done, but eventually it worked itself out.

Based on the letter of intent, the final contract is later finalized and we could begin working. It became a race against the clock to get everything done in time because we could only stay out on the Barentsz Sea until September. After that the weather would become too unpredictable and the chance to salvage the Kursk in 2001 would become very small.

According to the contract entered into with Rubin all materials had to be tested in advance. Many of the tests were performed in Holland on the shipyard where the Giant 4 and the sawing pontoon were built. But the grippers that were to be attached under the skin of the Kursk to lift her had to be tested in Russia at the Krylov Institute. I had to be present there and was transported to the testing grounds by a van. The site was fenced off with barbed wire, walls and was heavily guarded. Later I understood that Westerners never came here, let alone to talk about technical information. It was, of course, all a military secret. I saw scale models from out of the cold war and in the meeting room there was both a black and a red telephone. At such a moment you start asking yourself questions.

Rubin thought this test was so important that they broadcast the results on Russian television. Had we failed, then the project could not have been completed because of the severe time pressures. In the meantime, the grippers were already in production. That puts enormous pressure on you.

Around midnight it was concluded that the test was a success and we were treated to vodka and caviar.

Furthermore, the steering software for the heave compensation system had to be tested and the people that were going to operate them needed intensive training. The test went as follows: somebody would set in the weight of the Kursk and the operation crew had to individually set the 26 lifting points without knowing what the weight was and where the center of gravity was located. And which part of the Kursk was filled with water? And was it the suction effect on the sea floor or was it real weight? We could do all of this extensive practicing with the computer, even while the Giant 4 was on its way from Amsterdam to Kirkenes. In doing so we discovered a tiny omission and

Wessel Helmens during a meeting in the crew quarters on the Giant 4.

the Norwegians made a helicopter available to fly in a programmer from the German company that made the software. At moments like those you see how important a good preparation is for an operation.

When we arrived in Kirkenes, we couldn't sail out because of bad weather. That gave us time to further work out a couple of details, amongst those the re-entry system that was needed to get the grippers lowered to 100 meter (330 feet) depth through the holes that were cut in the Kursk. You have to imagine that that was the only thing, together with the working of the heave compensation system that we could really only try-out on-site and then it also had to work well immediately.

The weather had given us a lot of trouble and caused unavoidable delays. I still remember very well that we had to safely lock everything into position during heavy storms and had to slacken the cables of the then already attached grippers, because the heave compensation system had a margin of 3 meters (10 feet) and we were confronted with swings of more than 6 meters (20 feet). There was a spooky atmosphere prevalent onboard.

The grippers were hanging loose in the pipes. The Giant 4 lay diagonally and was rolling on the waves, which made it seem as if there was an alarm bell clanging. When you walked over the vessel, you heard the "klunk" through the whole Giant 4, kept into place with the help of the mooring cables. If they would give way, then it probably was curtains for the salvage job. When lying in bed, we slept just beside the mooring cables, you could hear them squeak. I still hear that sound every now and then...

Still, I never doubted that we could get the Kursk up. After the first gripper was attached, I knew it would work. The wind direction was regularly a spoilsport. Although the sea was flat the heave could be very large. The Kursk was laying on the shallowest point in the surrounding area, on a small hill, and that caused much more damming up of the water. Wind coming from the south was the best for us.

"...I never doubted that we could get the Kursk up. After the first gripper was attached, I knew it would work..."

In the beginning, because of the bad weather, we could only get the grippers into the holes very slowly. But when the weather cleared up, we made it into a contest to see how fast we could insert them. We had to recover a lot of lost time and that was good for morale. To give you an example: the first gripper took more than a day, but eventually we reached a record of 10 grippers a day. As soon as all grippers were attached, we could begin lifting. When we were moored in Murmansk Harbor, we could finally get off the ship. But the weather turned very cold, about -8 degrees Celsius (17 degrees Fahrenheit). Luckily there were several Russian seamen that offered to sell us their warm, fur-covered hats. That offer took off like a raging forest fire and quickly the offer was bigger than the demand.

The docking gave us more problems than expected because of stability issues around the pontoons Mar and Gon. The crew was deathly tired and many colleagues had the flu. The enormous pressure was removed from the steaming kettle, because the Kursk had been raised. The docking, however, would unfortunately take much longer than we hoped.

This caused us to return to Holland much later. When the flight was booked we had to go all the way to Kirkenes, although sailing to Murmansk would only take an hour. The shores were closer but that was all restricted military territory, so we were not allowed to pass through it. I was almost killed in an accident on my way to Kirkenes. The boat arrived very late and I had to be at the border post between Russia and Norway by 9:00 p.m. There is absolutely nothing there, it is the middle of nowhere and pitch dark blackness everywhere. The cab driver, with no snow tires or chains around the wheels, made his move at 100 km per hour (60 mph) on land roads that you could hardly see anymore through the snow. I underwent this ride from Hell together with a diver from Smit and thought; "We're not leaving this country alive". It was a death ride, a kind of Paris-Dakar rally without headlights across snowcovered tundra. Then the cab driver stopped on a very slippery stretch of road. He spoke a little English, was very religious and said: "I always get out here to pray at a little chapel". At that moment, I heard a Russian choir singing, in the vicinity of that tiny village. I am a religious person too and that moment of silence was, for me, a very appropriate ending to the whole adventure.

A short time later we got in the car and continued the ride. At the border there was a bus with Russians waiting in front of us but the cab driver told we were from Mammoet and then we could proceed immediately. The next day, after more than 6 weeks, I could embrace my family again.

Left: The client is always in the neighborhood.

Middle: Wessel Helmens in a conversation with people from Rubin and the Russian Navy.

Right: Preparing for docking.

The salvagers and the stay-at-homes use E-mail to keep in touch.

06-10-'01

W.Helmens

Van: "giant 4"< giant4@mail.station_12.com >
Aan: "W.Helmens"< whelmens@chello.nl >
Verzonden: woensdag 3 oktober 2001 21:42

Lieve Myraim,

Hier dan eindelijk weer eenst een bericht uit de Barentz zee.

Bedank voor jullie e-mailtjes.

Heeft Wouter z'n scooter al? Hij moet natuurlijk eerst nog z'n rijbewijs hal

Slaapt Tanja lekker op de grond?

Klaas Lamphen

Name Klaas Lamphen

Age 46

Function Director Product Development

Role in the Project Responsible for the development of techniques

Number of service years to Mammoet 11

After Jan van Seumeren, Wessel Helmens and I came back from St. Petersburg, I got to work developing the techniques. A lot of material would have to be specially designed and built for the salvage operation. Although it's been an incredibly complex project you often get ideas for the execution by looking at things in daily life. I will give you an example. Every gripper, and there were in total 26, had to be provided with 54 strands, each one 150 meters (500 feet) in length, that had to be easily spooled up and down. If you add that all together, you get a mountain of spaghetti of more than 200 kilometers (120 miles) in length. You can't have that loose on deck. And you don't escape the problem by spooling them up vertically next to each other, because they are not allowed to become entangled with each other. I was pondering this problem in the garden when I saw my sons bicycle standing there. I looked at the hand brakes and suddenly I knew how it had to be done, with an inside and an outside cable. I immediately made a draft and a scale model with a couple of strands next to each other. It worked.

A lot of the product development work was done together with the Russians and various Dutch suppliers. Rubin is very knowledgeable but they are also very protective, after all they design super secret things for the Russian Navy. The basic idea of the cutting of the holes and the lowering of the grippers came to us from our Russian colleagues; they explained that to us when we were in St. Petersburg. Jan said immediately: "make contact with Arie de Zwart of Huisman". That is an airplane technician and in no time Arie returned faxes with the drawing of the grippers. The Russians found it great to see how quickly we shifted gears based on their information. Arie de Zwart was fed by the Russian ideas and after that has delivered a great design performance.
At first we wanted to lift the Kursk with the nose still attached, but Rubin did not want that, that was not an option. They wanted to know how we were going to solve that. In the hotel I called a friend, a former submarine

captain, and explained to him that we had to saw underwater. According to him that was no problem. He suggested driving two piles into the sea bottom and then letting two tugboats sail up and down with a sawing cable in between them. When we told that idea to the people of Rubin the next day in the meeting, they spontaneously started to applaud.

Afterwards this principle was adjusted and two suction anchors were chosen, a tested technique with which you pump out water which causes the anchors to suck themselves stuck. This way they can move well with the sawing cable. Otherwise the sawing angle becomes too large.

With the detailed engineering I mostly concentrated on the heave compensation system that had to neutralize the swell of the waves on the Barentsz Sea, the spools and the re-entry lines that would guide the 8 ton (18,000 pounds) heavy grippers to the bottom of the sea. The divers had already made holes there with a ring assembled on top of it on which these lines could be tied off.

For the testing I used an old piece of steel skin that resembled the skin of the Kursk. The Russians came to Holland to watch how we made the holes, lowered the grippers into them and then pulled them up again. Those frequent visits contributed a lot to the mutual understanding between the Russians and the Dutch and that made the cooperation at sea much easier.

From May, 2001 on it was a 7 days a week/16 hours per day enterprise. I was chief and engine of the assembly line. At Shipdock in Amsterdam I myself manufactured the first strandjack and pulled all the cables through. The people that walked with the spooling up of the cables have each walked a complete "Nijmegen four days walk" (the equivalent of more than 4 marathons).

When a lifting unit was ready, it was tipped over and placed on the Giant 4 with a big crane. The logistics on the Giant 4 had to continuously be monitored because it was like a witches brewing kettle. From everywhere in Holland components were delivered for the build-up. We also could not, of course, test everything to scale. For me it was

"I looked at the hand brakes and suddenly I knew how it should be done, with an inside and an outside cable."

an absolute highlight when the system was turned on upon the Barentsz Sea and all spools started running and worked flawlessly. After all was said and done, we worked something out that was used 3 months later. That was a terrific performance.

Klaas Lamphen at the shipyard

and on board the Giant 4.

On–the-spot improvements are being made.

Arjan Braspenning

Name Arjan Braspenning

Age 25

Function Technical Assistant

Role in the Project Technical support building up the Giant 4 and during operation at sea

Number of service years to Mammoet 5

The first assignment I had was the production of a test gripper. I did not realize then that it was for the Kursk. But that realization came quickly and before I knew it I had to show the gripper to the Russians that especially came to Holland for this.

From that moment on, I was almost continuously busy in Amsterdam at the assembly line for the build-up of the Giant 4. I put together a couple of grippers, assembled cylinders, checked hoses and attached the gripper plates. I also helped with the spooling up of the winching spools.

In total I spent 9 weeks and 1 day on the Giant 4 from her departure from Amsterdam until the arrival in Murmansk when the Kursk was hanging underneath. I had never before been on the sea so it was an enormous experience. The stories that I heard about the Barentsz Sea were worse than reality. For me, it turned out better than expected not counting the number of days when we had really bad weather.

Once the captain told us that there was a very heavy storm coming and we only had a couple of hours to lock everything down. For example, the two cranes on board had to be stored in their safe place, determined in advance. Next we had to collapse all of the masts flat and lock down the crane counterweights, otherwise the crane could slam itself overboard. We already had 4 grippers attached to the Kursk and those lines had to be loosened, because the heave compensation system could not neutralize the coming heave. That was being done from the computer room. Everything that could be lashed down was brought down to keep the top weight as low as possible. We had only 2 hours to get all that done and then everyone on board was cooperating at maximum speed. In total, we had to do that 5 times. A storm like that lasted for 2 days and then we had to untie everything again and set it back up.

The average age on board was 26 years. Jan van Seumeren later told a newspaper reporter that you can achieve a lot with young men. I think we showed that.

During the salvage operation I was atop of one of the lifting platforms and received instruction from the computer control room. It was 12 hours up, 12 hours down. People asked me what I did in the meantime. Well, there was no meantime, it was sleeping, working, eating. Everything had to be very precisely tuned-in between the day and night teams. If we weren't lifting, then there was maintenance, and there were help tools produced and continual on–the-spot improvements being made. After all, it was all being done for the first time.

When all grippers were finally inside the Kursk, I got the feeling it would be a success, we would get her. I didn't really notice her coming loose from the sea bottom, but when the Kursk hit the saddles under the Giant 4, I felt her shudder all over. They bumped three times against each other before the Kursk was pulled tight. Three blows of 15,000 tons - 48 million pounds (the Giant 4) and 9,000 tons - 20 million pounds (the Kursk) against each other. You then heard a very hollow thud. After that, the vessel became very quiet and the tension broke.

We could choose if we wanted to go home or stay on board to Murmansk. I wanted to also witness the docking so I stayed on the Giant 4. A couple of colleagues were replaced by new crewmembers. The docking turned out very badly because we had problems with the stability of the pontoons. That caused the process to last 2 weeks longer than we planned. I didn't regret a minute of it. I wouldn't have missed it for the world and I would immediately go again if there is another boat to be lifted.

The feeling that we also lifted up people I only realized when we entered Murmansk Harbor. All of the Russian boats started tooting their horns and then you swallow and realize that you have a mass grave hanging under the Giant 4. The laying of the wreath in the dock was very impressive. It was an adventure to never be forgotten.

"It was 12 hours up, 12 hours down. People asked me what I did in the meantime. Well, there was no meantime, it was sleeping, working, eating. Everything had to be very precisely tuned-in between the day and night teams."

Arjan Braspenning lowers the guided cable with the use of mono jacks (mini-strandjacks).

Arie de Zwart

Name Arie de Zwart

Age 37

Function Structural Engineer (Strength Calculations)

Role in the Project Development of the gripper, works for Huisman

Number of service years to Huisman-Itrec 9

Huisman has been building cranes for Mammoet for years and is a good acquaintance. When a telephone call came from Jan van Seumeren in Russia with the request to "quickly" deliver a design for a gripper, I immediately went to work with the help of my colleagues Dick Steinman and Erik Romein. One of the first things we did was go to the hardware store to get a couple of hollow wall plugs and look at them up close, because that really has been the basic principle to attach the grippers in and under the skin of the Kursk. My knowledge of airplane building came in handy thinking of the clamps that Fokker used to temporarily connect plates before they were fastened. The forces that would be exerted against the grippers would be very large, so we had to design an extremely compact construction.

On May 15th, 2001 we faxed the first design to Rubin and got it back a day later, with the necessary comments noted. Again we rapidly went to work and sent the changed design back on the same day. And another day later the newspapers announced that Mammoet won the assignment. That was not only because of our design but also because there had been such a quick and adequate response here and back. It was very important that we received correct information about the submarine because we had to take into account all kinds of preconditions. A gripper can only turn and spread open in free air. When you drill holes, no wires and other stuff should be in the way, so a very precise lay-out of the boat was required.

We had less than 1 month to produce 26 grippers, that all were just a little bit different because they had to be attached under the skin of the Kursk at a certain angle. One gripper weighs 4 tons so we had to form an enormous amount of steel in very little time. That in itself was a gigantic job. And during the design and testing stage we got again and again little pieces of new information that regularly led to new adjustments.

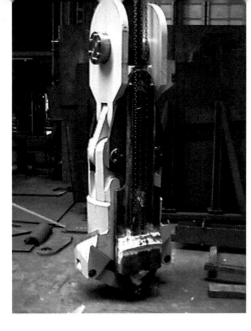

Test of the gripper in a simulated
piece of the Kursks hull.

The Russians demanded a testing version that would have twice the power that was needed. The holes in the
skin of the Kursk were allowed to be 700 millimeter (28 inches) in diameter maximally and the gripper had to
go through that. That was also about the limit.

Testing is extremely important. For illustration, we calculated that if a gripper should break away during lifting,
the energy that is released with that is enough to launch the platform of a strandjack 35 meters into the air, and
if that comes down... you don't even want to think about the consequences. That energy had to be compensated
for in the design. You can compare it with answering the question: "how do you stop a truck of 30 tons (67,000
pounds) that drives 20 kilometer an hour (12 mph) within 2 meters (6 feet)?" To be able to compensate for a
bang like that, of which we hoped would never happen, we designed a system of strips and steel wedges and
a very strong steel ring that would press together the pipe through which the strands of the strandjacks run.
That would be enough to slow down a break-away gripper.

For me the most important moment at the salvage was that the grippers were all placed and opened with the
little margin for error that we had. That's when I had the feeling that I did my work well. They were in!

Various power tests on the
gripper using a draw-bench.

Paul Glerum

Name Paul Glerum

Age 46

Function Salvage Inspector

Role in the Project Responsible for the final development
of the sawing system needed to saw off the nose of the Kursk

Working at the time of the salvage for Smit International for 25 years, now with Multraship

I already began working on the development of a sawing method when there was still mention that the consortium of Smit/Heerema/Halliburton would perform the salvage. When it became clear that Mammoet had won the assignment and would hire Smit for the maritime work, I was involved anew with the project.

The development of the sawing system was not yet totally finished and we still had to conduct a number of tests. At first we used a chain, but with test sawing it turned out that after 1.5 hours of sawing the cable was already broken. We were all in Kirkenes. The bad weather did not allow us to work on the site but it did give us extra time to improve the sawing cable. The saw cans were brought back to Holland by truck. Overthere they assembled chromium steel cans on it. 10 days later they were back in Kirkenes. With a new test we were able to increase sawing time to 6 hours. Also a subject of discussion were the suction anchors needed to steer the saw. They weigh 100 tons (224,000 pounds) each and you cannot place them overboard at open sea. In Kirkenes we had to already hang them on each side of the sawing vessel with the help of the cranes on board. Once securely fastened, we could sail to the place of doom on the Barentsz Sea to perform in reality what in theory had only been thought about.

The actual sawing of the nose took only 32 hours to complete, but in real time we needed more than four weeks on location. When the drive cable broke, the suction anchors had to go back up because they had to move with the sawing cable and make a maximum angle of 20 degrees. The first time the driving cable broke we were four days (!) busy repairing it. It was also the first time ever that moving anchors had been used for sawing.

"Once securely fastened, we could sail to the place of doom on the Barentsz Sea to perform in reality what in theory had only been thought about."

On the diving vessel Mayo, I could see on the monitors what the divers did below. They all had a camera on their helmet. Daily I sailed from the sawing ship to the Mayo and back in a rubber boat. I could hear through a speaker what the divers said to each other and then I would confer with the diving superintendent Wally Wallace on what we would have to do next.

The sawing cable had a length of 70 meters (225 feet) and with that we could make an effective movement of 90 meters (288 feet). The saw moved top-to-bottom with a speed of 60 meters (192 feet) per minute. The angle of 20 degrees was critical. The skin of the Kursk was made of high quality steel with high caliber carbon. If you apply too little pressure, the material starts hardening and then you cannot get through at all. The driving mechanism never failed during the operation. Only the cable breach and the bad weather haunted us. Eventually we sawed much more than we had planned. We sawed from top to bottom, amongst and through the anchor holder. The sawed through anchor chain pieces fell down which meant that we had to go through them time and again.. Also, we had to saw very close to a cruise missile through the middle of the torpedo tube. Theoretically it was possible that we could saw through the torpedo itself but thankfully that did not happen.

I was not fearful during the job. After the sawing I went back to Holland, my job was done, finished. I excitedly followed from a distance how the process went further but knew the preparations had been thorough enough.

Paul Glerum walks with a colleague through the plans

before the sawing vessel leaves for the place of doom.

The "altar" in Gonnie and Frans' house.

Gonnie van Seumeren

Name Gonnie van Seumeren

Role in the Project Wife, support and anchor of
Frans van Seumeren, name giver of the Russian pontoon Gon

I have really been involved with the project since the first conversation between Rubin and Mammoet. This was because Frans and I in January, 2001 were in Moscow, visiting with friends. On the day we wanted to go home, Frans got a telephone call to come to St. Petersburg and I went along. Throughout this I have experienced all of the first meetings and lived through it with Frans when it fell through later because Rubin was still thinking that the consortium of Smit/Heerema/Halliburton would perform the salvage operation.

A couple of months later the situation looked entirely different. We were on a holiday in Greece when Frans suddenly was called to a meeting in St. Petersburg. I did not go with him but flew back to Holland on the same day Frans came home with the assignment under his arm.

I was very proud of the fact that a "small" company from De Meern had gotten such an important assignment and the whole village empathized with us. From that moment on, our life was controlled by the Kursk day and night. In the preparation period I regularly joined Frans to watch the progress of the Giant 4's construction. My brother-in-law Jan then came up with the idea that the pontoons that were supposed to lift the Kursk and the Giant 4 combination into dry-dock, had to be named. They became the Mar, my sister in laws name is Marjorie, and the Gon. Through this we became even more involved with the salvage and in a very special way. To save time the pontoons were built in Russia at the PO Sevmash shipyard. When they were ready, we were invited to come and christen them. The Mar was first into the water and the Gons turn came three weeks later.

I have saved as a treasured keepsake, the neck of the champagne bottle I threw against the Gon. Some time later things were not going well on the Barentsz Sea, it was horrifically bad weather and Frans had to go there.

Before he left, he asked if I wanted to light a candle of which the flame should stay burning until the salvage was completed. I erected a little altar and put next to it all kinds of things and pictures that were related to the salvage project. For the candle I bought a big glass bell jar and stocked up a fairly big supply of candles. In that last difficult and very tense period this was a place for me in the house where I could come for some reflection.

I always maintained confidence in the success of the whole undertaking and when the Kursk finally was safely lying in the dock I extinguished the candle. With that the project for us, however, was still far from being completed. After everybody was back, a media circus burst loose. Mammoet was awarded several important honors. Some were personal and others, like the King William I prize, were for the entire company.

Next to it all, I had an ongoing sense that there were deceased people in the Kursk. That is why I regret that I wasn't given the opportunity to meet with the surviving family members. I wanted to give them a sense that we have great empathy for having lived through the whole experience with them and that we realize that their family members have been brought home.

A solemn moment for all engaged, after 9 weeks of work ruled by a very tight time-limit.

The media were fully represented at the christening of the first pontoon the Mar. The pontoon is named after the wife of Jan van Seumeren, Marjorie.

Gonnie and Frans van Seumeren stand amidst the employees of the Russian shipbuilders PO Sevmash.

After a blessing from an Orthodox priest, the 100 meter long (330 feet), 15 meter wide (almost 50 feet) and 9 meter high (30 feet) Gon is ready to leave.

Igor Spassky

Name Igor Spassky

Age 75

Function President of The Rubin Company

Role in the Project Principal, bearing final responsibility on behalf of Rubin

Number of service years to Rubin 53

Igor Spassky, seaman in heart and soul, was on behalf of the Russian government, the principal for the raising of the Kursk. He has a long and impressive career building for the Russian Navy. After as a young man in the Navy Academy in St. Petersburg being promoted to engineering, he entered the Russian Navy and was stationed on a cruiser in the Black Sea. It was during a time that Russia decided to drastically reinforce her Navy. One of the effects of that decision was the expansion of the design bureau Rubin. In 1950 Spassky was seconded to Rubin by the Russian Navy. From that moment on his life was synonymous with submarines. In 1968 a promotion to head of the engineering department followed and with that Spassky became the number two in command at Rubin. 8 years later, in 1974, he got the top job in the Bureau, a function he still holds.

In an exclusive interview given in St. Petersburg, he looks back on the salvage operation. This interview can

 be found on the DVD in the back of this book.

During one of his visits in Holland,
Spassky explains to the personal assistent
of Putin, Sergey Yastrzhembskiy,
the operation of the grippers.

Spassky had to put his signature many
times on important documents before
and during the whole project.

09:28:21 THS 041 U 10/23/01

Victor Baranov

Name Victor Baranov

Age 69

Function Head of engineering at Rubin, designer of the Kursk

Role in the Project Technically responsible for the salvage operation

Number of service years to Rubin 47

Victor Baranov was born and raised in Tashkent, where no sea can be found. As a young man he devoured the books of Jules Verne and fell in love with the sea. After his high school exams, he left for St. Petersburg, known then still as Leningrad, and enlisted in the Navy Academy. A medical test revealed that he was short-sighted and he was turned down for active duty. This first taste of defeat did not slow him; he enrolled in the Leningrad Shipbuilding Institute where he was accepted. In 1956 he successfully graduated and began working that same year at Rubin as an engineer and designer. He progressed in the succeeding years to the head of engineering and is now still the second man of the Bureau, behind Igor Spassky. In opposition to a couple of his study friends that have been retired already for several years, he still designs submarines and has sailed on many of them in his working life. Although not a Navy Officer, he sees the sea as his natural environment.

Baranov was also willing to exclusively appear in front of the cameras. From his point of view and involvement, he describes afterwards his experiences during the salvage operation. This interview is also included on the DVD in the back of the book.

DVD

Baranov and Ovdienko on board the Giant 4

in the harbor of Roslyakovo.

Igor Ovdienko

Name Igor Ovdienko

Age 39

Function Engineer and designer at Rubin

Role in the Project Partially responsible for assessing the salvage plan;
project leader at the preparation stage as well as the salvage stage on the Barentsz Sea.

Number of service years to Rubin 17

Igor Ovdienko graduated in 1986 from the Leningrad Shipbuilding Institute after studying maritime architecture
and related subjects. The most important of those was the designing and building of submarines. During his
studies as a cadet, he visited various submarines. Almost immediately after his graduation he started at Rubin.
In the past 15 years he has tested many submarines, sailed with them and handed them over to the Russian Navy.
Some of them were of the Oscar II class. For Ovdienko, the salvage operation was in many ways very emotional.
It was not only the salvage operation that moved him deeply, he was also personally involved in it because some
of his old study friends sailed on that last disastrous journey of the Kursk.

In an openhearted interview, Ovdienko tells what he went through, from the announcement of the sinking until
the homecoming in Murmansk. This interview is also exclusively included on the DVD in the back of this book.

Igor Ovdienko knew Oscar II type submarines like the Kursk inside and out. For that
reason he was completely indispensable to
this project.

Anna Skorokhodova

Name Anna Skorokhodova

Age 42

Function Interpreter-translator

Role in the Project Led the group of interpreters and translators.
Personal Assistant to Igor Spassky.

Number of service years to Rubin 12

Anna Skorokhodova started her studies at the Electro-technical College in St. Petersburg in 1978. She was educated there as a translator of technical literature and scientific books and as an electro-technician. Before she was hired by Rubin as a full-time interpreter-translator in 1991, she worked at the Admiralty Shipyard, also in St. Petersburg. She was continuously involved in the project from the first negotiations until the homecoming of the Kursk to Murmansk Harbor. And she has, just like Slava Zakharov, played a very important role in helping the Russians and the Dutch successfully work together. Her husband, also working at Rubin, actively participated in determining the cause of the disaster after the Kursk was salvaged.

In the interview on the DVD in the back of this book, Anna looks back on the operation and tells how complex it was every now and then to grow the level of understanding on both sides of the table during the negotiations.

During her work in Holland,
Anna Skorokhodova beholds with
her own eyes the progress of
the Giant 4 in Amsterdam.

Slava Zakharov

Name Slava Zakharov

Age 46

Function Director Mammoet Russia

Role in the Project Liaison officer between Rubin and Mammoet

Number of service years to Mammoet 8

Slava Zakharov finished high school in 1974 and went into the military service as a soldier and then later as a sergeant. After his tour of duty he studied in Moscow with the Institute for engineering and construction and was educated as a designer and builder. He found a job in the Ministry of Energy as the head of the mechanical department. There he gained experience working with large salvage cranes and he became, because he spoke English very well, involved in negotiations with foreign companies. In 1993 this worked out well for him, because the ministry needed to sell a couple of large cranes since during that time there was not enough work in Russia. One of the companies that expressed interested in the sale was Mammoet, then still called Van Seumeren. Zakharov met Frans van Seumeren in Voronezh. That was the start of a cooperation that would last until 1995. In that year he was offered a job at Van Seumeren and from that day on Zakharov set-up an office for the enterprise that he successfully leads.

In the interview on the DVD in the back of this book, Zakharov describes how he made the initial contacts with Rubin for Mammoet, was actively involved in the negotiations and jumped in during the salvage project wherever needed. Zakharovs contribution was essential for forging the basis of the trust bond that developed between the Russians and the Dutch.

A deeply moved Zakharov, the moment the Kursk is loosened from the sea bottom.

Wally Wallace

Name Wally Wallace

Age 55

Funtion Diving Superintendent

Role in the Project Supervising and instructing
the divers from the diving vessel Mayo

Number of service years to Subsea 7 (recently formed as a result of a combination
of *Halliburton Subsea* and the subsea activities of *DSND subsea ASA*) 4

In the mid 1960s, Wally Wallace began his diving training in the British Army. When the exploitation of the oil
fields in the North Sea began in the 1970s, Wallace decided to go into commercial diving. During more than
10 years he worked as a professional diver onboard oil drilling rigs. In 1981 he was appointed off-shore manager
and supervisor. His most important task is the inspection of oilfield constructions. When he was asked to work
on the Kursk project, he did not hesitate for a moment. It was an entirely new experience for him to work on
a salvage project.

In the interview on the DVD he explains how he communicated with the divers on the sea bottom and how
they operated during the operation.

From the diving vessel Mayo,
Wally Wallace directs the underwater works.

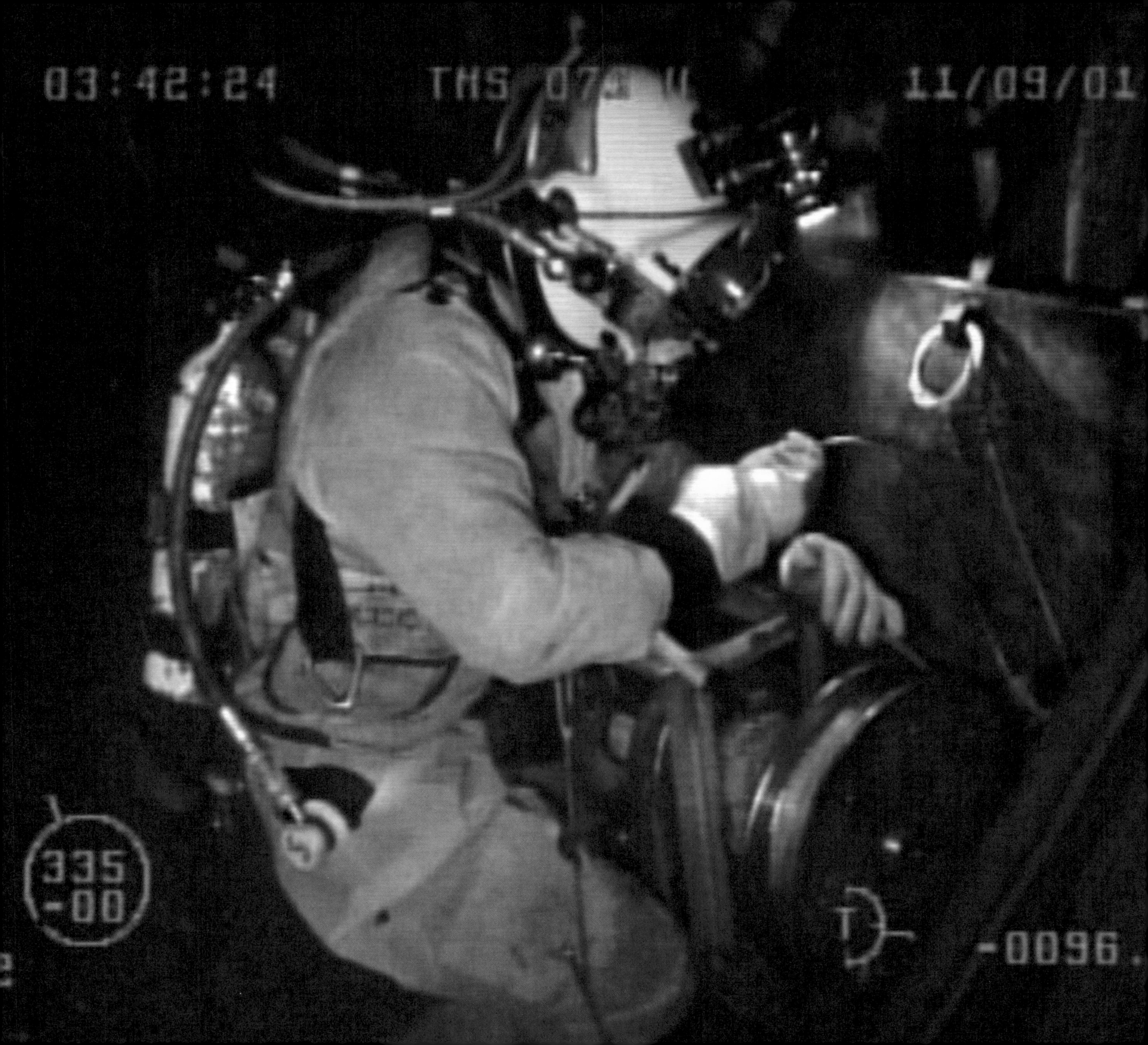
03:42:24
11/09/01
335
-00
-0096.

Jimmy Irvine

Name Jimmy Irvine

Age 51

Funtion Diver

Role in the Project Cutting the holes in the skin
of the Kursk and assisting in fastening the grippers

Number of service years to Subsea 7 (recently formed as a result of a combination
of *Halliburton Subsea* and the subsea activities of *DSND subsea ASA*) 4

Jimmy was born on the Shetland Islands where he had his first diving experience when he drove his car into the
sea after an accident. He borrowed diving equipment from a friendly islander and succeeded in rescuing the vehicle
all by himself. That success made him feel so good that he decided to make a living out of diving. After a study
as a civil technician he was all-in. Like Wally Wallace, he moved to offshore industries in the 1970s, and got
involved in deep-sea construction and raising operations. The raising of the Kursk was a welcome change for him
from the moderately routine work on board drilling rigs. On the DVD Jimmy tells exclusively about his experiences
at the bottom of the Barentsz Sea and his protracted stay on board the Mayo.

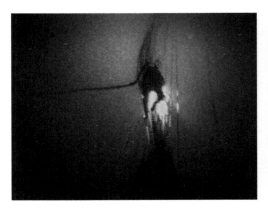  

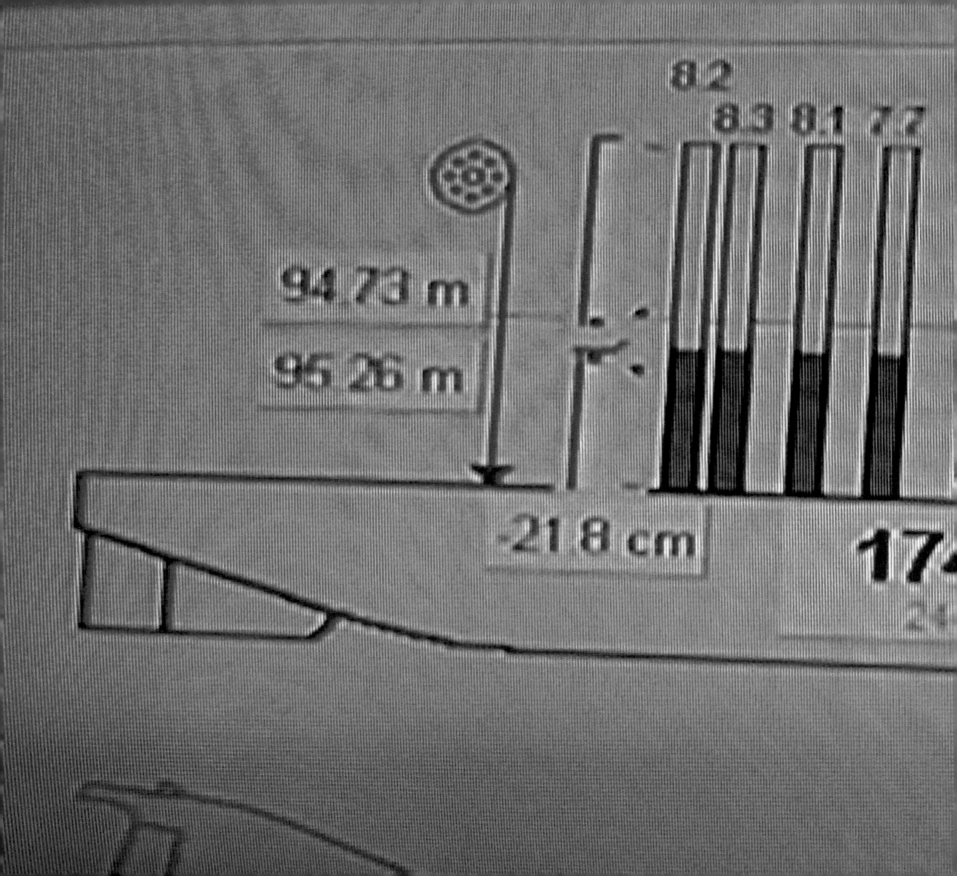

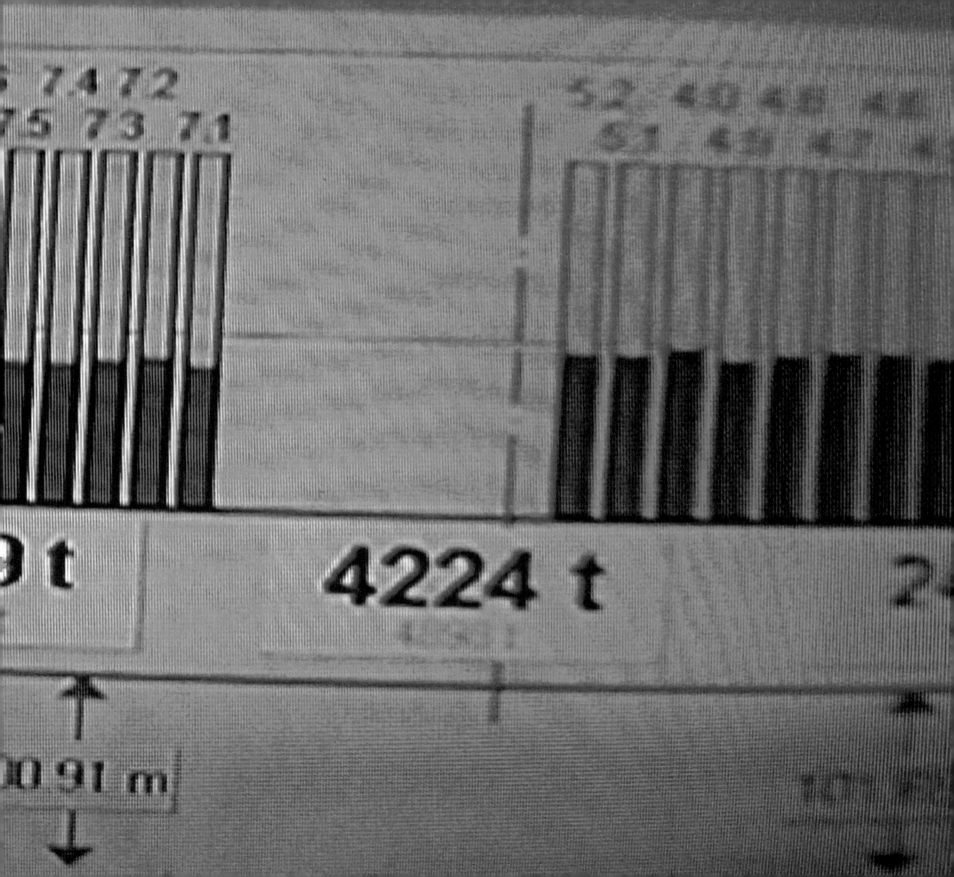

Part 3 - **The Technical Specifications**

Planning

Overall planning

RECOVERY OF THE KURSK

MAMMOET

ID	Pay No.	Task Name	Start	Duration	Fir
1		**Commercial Milestones**	18/05/01	129 days	24/0
2		Contract Award	18/05/01	0 days	18/0
3		Receive advance payment / submit guarantee	25/05/01	0 days	25/0
4		**STAGE I**	28/05/01	118 days	22/0
5	1	DESIGN WORK	12/06/01	102 days	22/0
6	1.1	Basic design completed	12/06/01	0 days	12/0
7	1.2 + 1.3	Experimental and Detailed design work completed	01/08/01	0 days	01/0
8	1.4	Engineering support completed	22/09/01	0 days	22/0
9	2	PREPARATORY WORK	28/05/01	111 days	15/0
10	2.1	Order(s) for Purchase of components for lifting system	28/05/01	9 days	05/0
11	2.2	Order for modification of the Lifting barge	28/05/01	19 days	15/0
12	2.3	Order for Pontoon manufacture	05/06/01	0 days	05/0
13	2.4	Finish of Diving Vessel outfitting and departure to sea	08/07/01	0 days	08/0
14	2.5	Completion of pontoon manufacture	15/09/01	0 days	15/0
15	3	UNDER WATER WORKS	29/07/01	44 days	10/0
16	3.1	Completion of work site survey, installation cutting equipment, washing out of s	29/07/01	0 days	29/0
17	3.2	Cutting out of Compartment 1	07/08/01	0 days	07/0
18	3.3	20% of hole(s) cutting completed	13/08/01	0 days	13/0
19	3.3	20% of hole(s) cutting completed	20/08/01	0 days	20/0
20	3.3	20% of hole(s) cutting completed	27/08/01	0 days	27/0
21	3.3	20% of hole(s) cutting completed	03/09/01	0 days	03/0
22	3.3	20% of hole(s) cutting completed	10/09/01	0 days	10/0
23		**STAGE II**	15/09/01	9 days	24/0
24	1	Installation of lifting units (hook on to ship)	15/09/01	0 days	15/0
25	2	Ship lifting with soil washing (if required)	18/09/01	0 days	18/0
26	3	Securing the ship under the barge	19/09/01	0 days	19/0
27	4	Transportation to the dock	20/09/01	0 days	20/0
28	5	Installation and securing support pontons to liftbarge	22/09/01	0 days	22/0
29	6	Installation of the ship into the floating dock	24/09/01	0 days	24/0
30	7	Equipment demobilised from Russia	24/09/01	0 days	24/0
31		**Execution (based on 20 lift Units)**	26/05/01	136 days	08/1
32		**STAGE I**	26/05/01	108 days	10/0
33		Testing (in Russia)	26/05/01	41 days	05/0
34		Engineering	26/05/01	10 days	04/0
35		Preparation hull test submarine, scale models	26/05/01	15 days	09/0
36		Pulling test	03/07/01	1 day	03/0
37		Cutting hole test (if required)	04/07/01	1 day	04/0
38		Sawing hull test (if required)	05/07/01	1 day	05/0
39		Nautical tests sailing with barge / subm	10/06/01	3 days	12/0
40		PREPARATION WORK SITE	27/05/01	107 days	10/0
41		Engineering	27/05/01	21 days	17/0
42		Fabrication special tools	17/06/01	21 days	08/0
43		Mobilization Diving vessel	08/07/01	5 days	13/0

Task	▭	Milestone ◼
Split		Summary ◼▬
Progress	▬▬	Rolled Up Task ▬

State Customer: Ministry of Defense of the Russian Federation

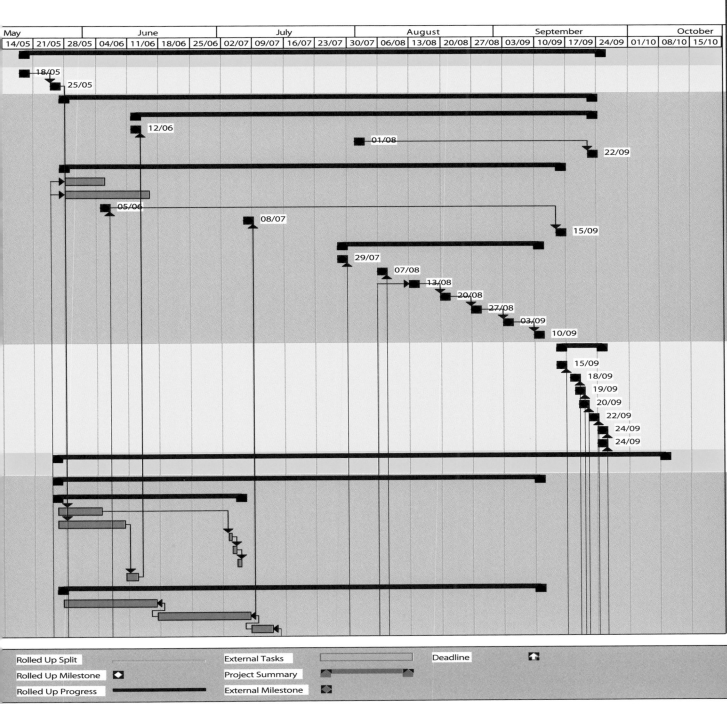

	Rolled Up Split		External Tasks		Deadline	
Rolled Up Milestone		Project Summary			
Rolled Up Progress		External Milestone			

Customer: Central Design Bureau for Marine Engineering "RUBIN"

Planning

Overall planning, continued

MAMMOET

ID	Pay No.	Task Name	Start	Duration	Fi
44		Survey work area	13/07/01	2 days	15/(
45		Soil removal	15/07/01	4 days	19/(
46		Installation cutting machine	19/07/01	10 days	29/(
47		Cutting front end of Submarine	29/07/01	9 days	07/(
48		Cutting 20 lift holes	07/08/01	35 days	10/(
49		STAGE II	26/05/01	136 days	08/(
50		Main Barge	26/05/01	107 days	09/(
51		Main Engineering	26/05/01	7 days	01/(
52		Purchasing modification works	26/05/01	24 days	18/(
53		Detail Engineering	02/06/01	28 days	29/(
54		Main modifications	30/06/01	42 days	10/(
55		20 jacking tubes	30/06/01	42 days	10/(
56		4 support barge connection points	30/06/01	42 days	10/(
57		Hole in barge for the sail	30/06/01	42 days	10/(
58		Transport saddles / Seafastening	30/06/01	42 days	10/(
59		Rigging 2 assist cranes	28/07/01	2 days	29/(
60		Installation Heave Compensator Assemblies	05/08/01	22 days	26/(
61		Pre installation Jacking Assemblies	16/08/01	11 days	26/(
62		Installation Mooring System	30/07/01	5 days	03/(
63		Installation Contingency Ballasting System	04/08/01	5 days	08/(
64		Survey / Certification and preparation voyage to Russia	26/08/01	1 day	26/(
65		Sail to Work Site	27/08/01	14 days	09/(
66		Lift System	26/05/01	84 days	17/(
67		Heave Compensator Assembly	26/05/01	84 days	17/(
68		Main Engineering	26/05/01	14 days	08/(
69		Detail Engineering	09/06/01	28 days	06/(
70		Purchasing main components	26/05/01	14 days	08/(
71		Delivery main components	23/06/01	56 days	17/(
72		Strand jack assembly (900 ton)	26/05/01	58 days	22/(
73		Main Engineering	26/05/01	5 days	30/(
74		Detail Engineering	31/05/01	15 days	14/(
75		Purchasing additional jacks strands wedges etc.	26/05/01	14 days	08/(
76		Purchasing 80 15 ton guy jacks	26/05/01	14 days	08/(
77		Delivery, collecting and maintenance	23/06/01	15 days	07/(
78		Testing	08/07/01	15 days	22/(
79		Mooring system	26/05/01	51 days	15/(
80		Main Engineering	26/05/01	10 days	04/(
81		Detail Engineering	05/06/01	20 days	24/(
82		Purchasing winches, wires and anchors	26/05/01	14 days	08/(
83		Delivery	07/07/01	7 days	13/(
84		Testing	14/07/01	2 days	15/(
85		Contingency Ballasting system	26/05/01	36 days	30/(
86		Main Engineering	26/05/01	10 days	04/(
87		Detail Engineering	05/06/01	20 days	24/(
88		Maintenance	25/06/01	5 days	29/(

Task		Milestone
Split		Summary
Progress		Rolled Up Task

State Customer: Ministry of Defense of the Russian Federation

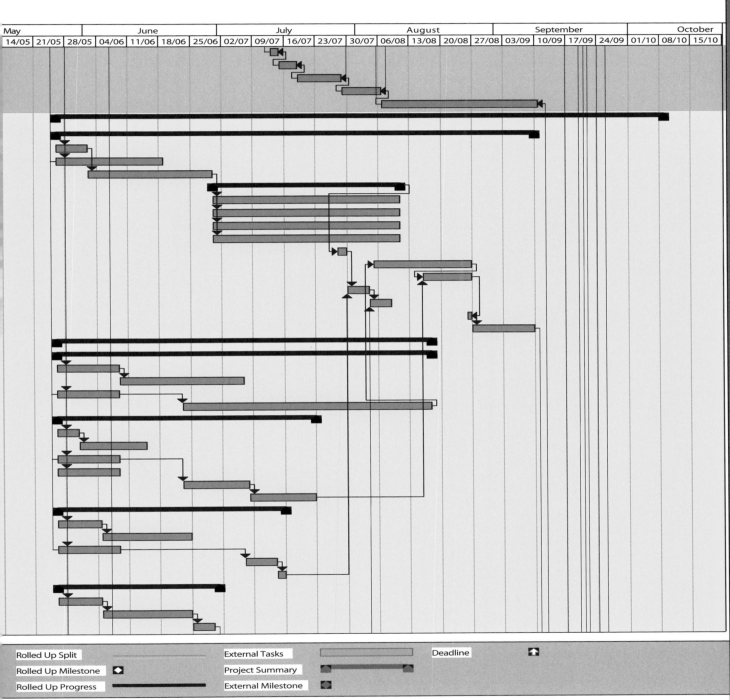

Rolled Up Split
Rolled Up Milestone
Rolled Up Progress

External Tasks
Project Summary
External Milestone

Deadline

Customer: Central Design Bureau for Marine Engineering "RUBIN"

Planning

Overall planning, continued

MAMMOET   RECOVERY OF THE KURSK

ID	Pay No.	Task Name	Start	Duration	Fir
89		Testing	30/06/01	1 day	30/0
90		Support Barges	26/05/01	117 days	19/0
91		Main Engineering	26/05/01	7 days	01/0
92		Finalise Contract	05/06/01	1 day	05/0
93		Detail Engineering	02/06/01	28 days	29/0
94		Fabrication	16/06/01	90 days	13/0
95		Transfer barges to Moermansk	14/09/01	6 days	19/0
96		MAIN LIFT PERIOD	10/09/01	11 days	20/0
97		Mooring barge in correct position	10/09/01	1 day	10/0
98		Installation Jacking Assemblies	11/09/01	4 days	14/0
99		Hook on Submarine	12/09/01	4 days	15/0
100		Final check and testing	16/09/01	2 days	17/0
101		LIFT SUBMARINE FROM BOTTOM	18/09/01	1 day	18/0
102		Fixation Submarine to Lift barge	19/09/01	1 day	19/0
103		Sail to Moermansk	20/09/01	1 day	20/0
104		ARRIVAL MOERMANSK	20/09/01	0 days	20/0
105		TRANSFER SUBMARINE INTO DOCK	21/09/01	18 days	08/1
106		Installation of 2 Support barges	21/09/01	2 days	22/0
107		Lift Mainbarge + Submarine above dock level	23/09/01	0.5 days	23/0
108		Move Barge assembly + Sub into dock	23/09/01	0.5 days	23/0
109		Jacking down submarine onto dock stools	24/09/01	1 day	24/0
110		Demobilisation of all Equipment	25/09/01	14 days	08/1

Task		Milestone	
Split		Summary	
Progress		Rolled Up Task	

State Customer: Ministry of Defense of the Russian Federation

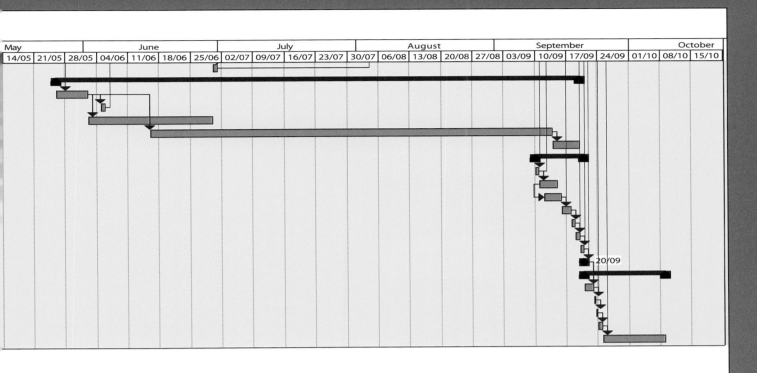

	May			June				July				August				September			October		
	14/05	21/05	28/05	04/06	11/06	18/06	25/06	02/07	09/07	16/07	23/07	30/07	06/08	13/08	20/08	27/08	03/09	10/09	17/09	24/09	01/10	08/10	15/10

20/09

Rolled Up Split	External Tasks	Deadline
Rolled Up Milestone	Project Summary	
Rolled Up Progress	External Milestone	

Customer: Central Design Bureau for Marine Engineering "RUBIN"

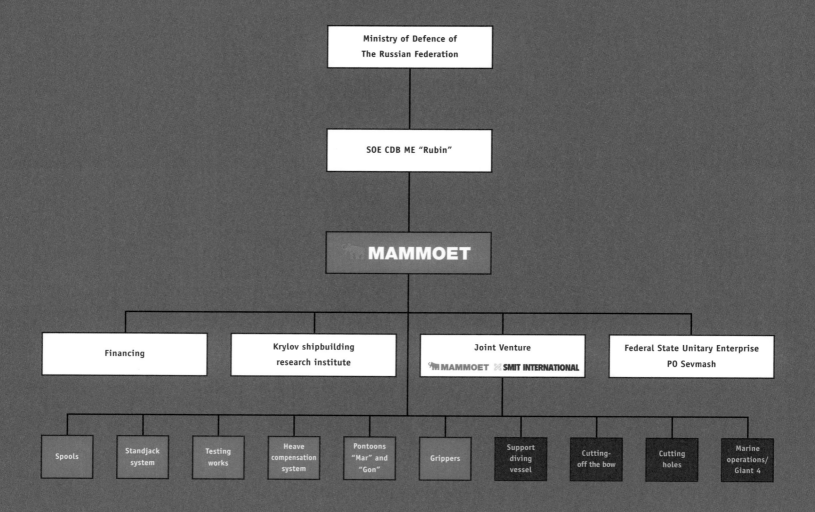

Spools

Strandjack system

Testing works

Heave compensation system

Pontoons "Mar" and "Gon"

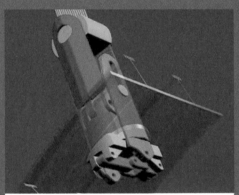

Grippers

Support diving vessel

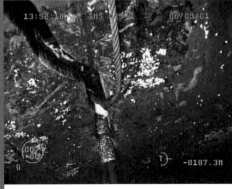

Cutting-off the bow

Cutting holes

Core Information Kursk

Proportional Scale Kursk

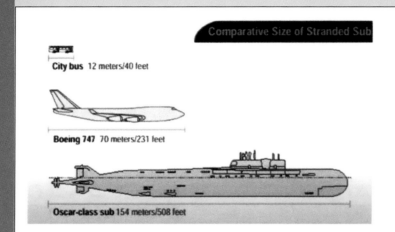

Comparative Size of Stranded Sub

City bus 12 meters/40 feet

Boeing 747 70 meters/231 feet

Oscar-class sub 154 meters/508 feet

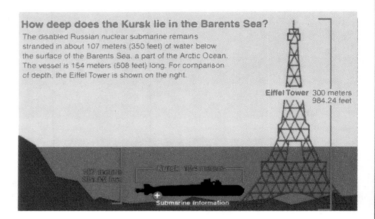

How deep does the Kursk lie in the Barents Sea?

The disabled Russian nuclear submarine remains stranded in about 107 meters (350 feet) of water below the surface of the Barents Sea, a part of the Arctic Ocean. The vessel is 154 meters (508 feet) long. For comparison of depth, the Eiffel Tower is shown on the right.

Eiffel Tower 300 meters
984.24 feet

Submarine Information

Side view of the Kursk

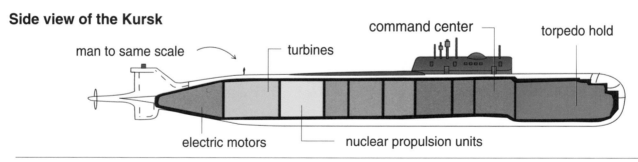

man to same scale

turbines

command center

torpedo hold

electric motors

nuclear propulsion units

Length: 155m	**Minimum draft:** 9,2m	**Weight:** 18.000 tonnes
Width: 18,2m	**Displacement:** 24.000 tonnes (under water)	**Power:** 190 megawatt per reactor

Sketches and Drawings

Cut-Away Views Kursk

~6 knots

~1st explosion - loss of fwd buoyancy

Loss of fwd buoyancy tank - fire in № 1 compartment

1st explosion - loss of buoyancy

~6 knots

outer casing and buoyancy tank debris from 1st explosion

2nd explosion - 2 to 5 tonnes TNT equivalent

135 seconds

PORT SIDE VIEW

STARBOARD SIDE VIEW

TOPVIEW SUPERSTRUCTURE

Sketches and Drawings

1st Idea

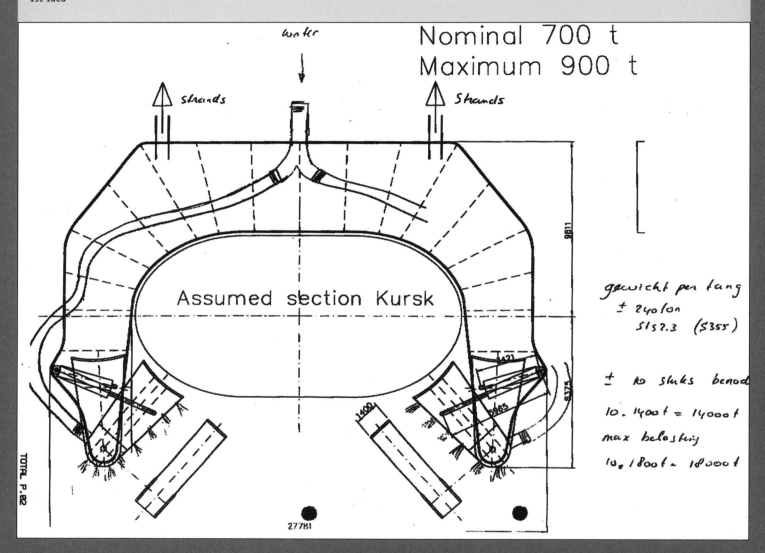

Sketches and Drawings

2nd Idea with bands under the Kursk

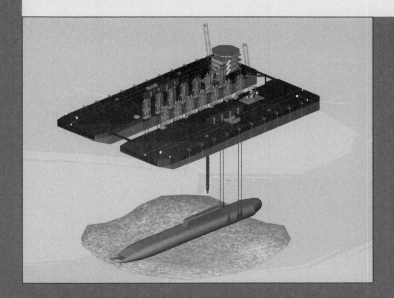

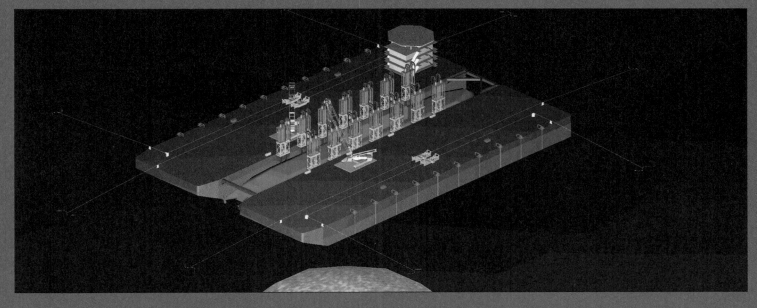

Sketches and Drawings

3rd Idea

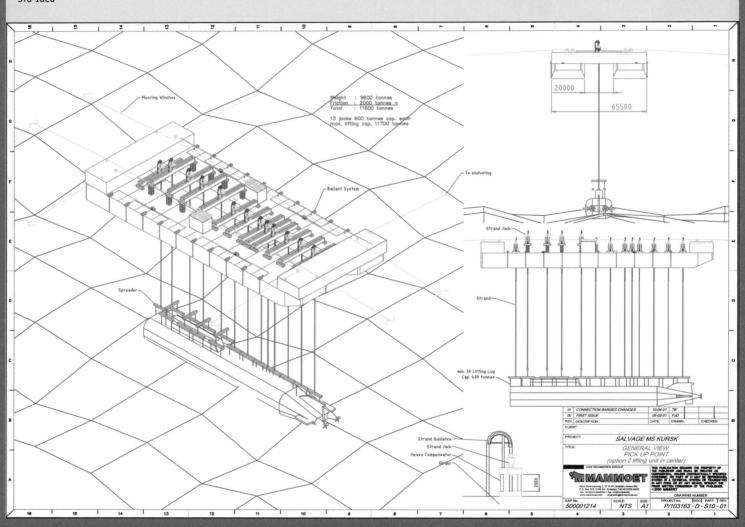

Weight　: 9600 tonnes
Friction : 2000 tonnes +
Total　 : 11600 tonnes

13 jacks 900 tonnes cap. each
max. lifting cap. 11700 tonnes

Mooring Winches

Ballast System

To anchoring

Strand Jack

Strand

Spreader

min. 30 Lifting Lug
Cap. 600 tonnes

20000

65500

Strand Guidance
Strand Jack
Heave Compensator
Girder

01	CONNECTION BARGES CHANGES	10-04-01	TB		
00	FIRST ISSUE	05-02-01	PJD		
REV.	DESCRIPTION:	DATE:	DRAWN:		CHECKED:

CLIENT:

PROJECT: **SALVAGE MS KURSK**

TITLE: *GENERAL VIEW PICK UP POINT (option 2 lifting unit in center)*

MAMMOET
VAN SEUMEREN GROUP

| SAP No: 500001214 | SCALE: NTS | SIZE: A1 | PROJECT No: P/103163 - D - S10 - 01 | DOC: | PART: | REV: |

Sketches and Drawings

Definive idea. However, during the operation - after tests at the Krylov Institute - it is decided that the Kursk will be connected under the Giant 4 back-to-front

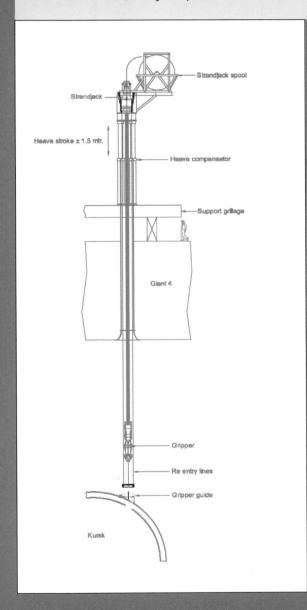

Strandjack spool

Strandjack

Heave stroke ± 1.5 mtr.

Heave compensator

Support grillage

Giant 4

Gripper

Re entry lines

Gripper guide

Kursk

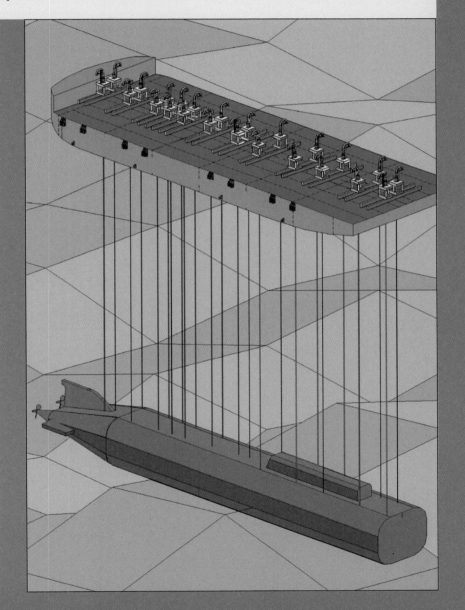

Sketches and Drawings

Lay-out of the Giant 4

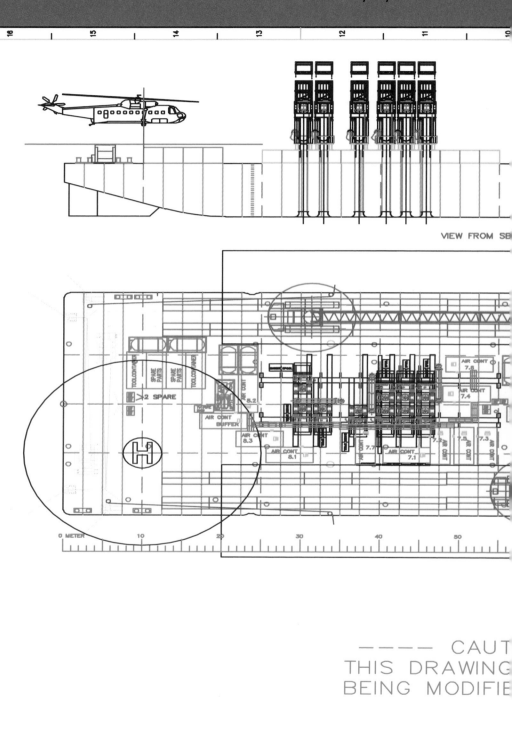

VIEW FROM SB

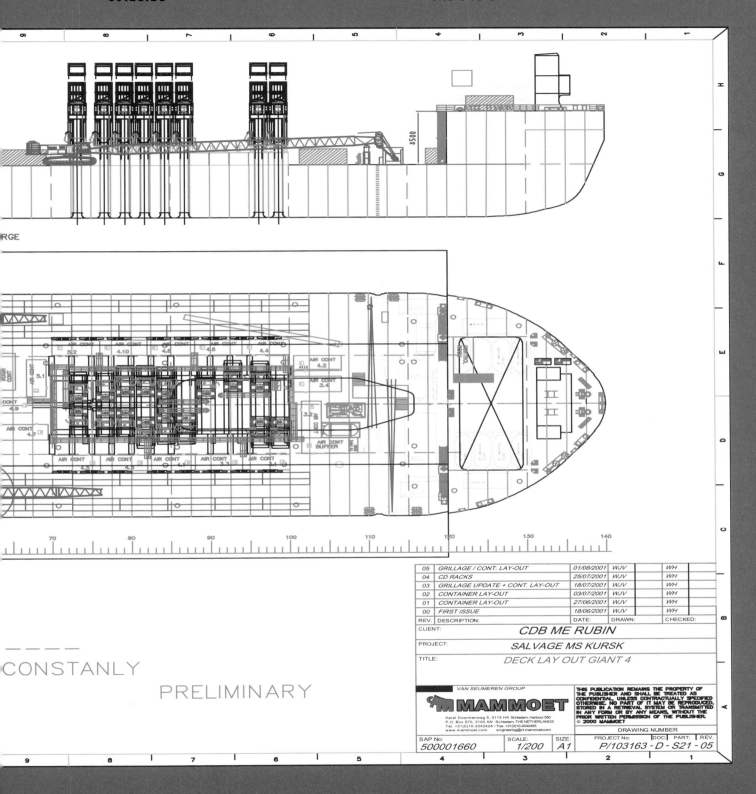

RGE

CONSTANLY

PRELIMINARY

05	GRILLAGE / CONT. LAY-OUT	01/08/2001	WJV	WH	
04	CD RACKS	25/07/2001	WJV	WH	
03	GRILLAGE UPDATE + CONT. LAY-OUT	18/07/2001	WJV	WH	
02	CONTAINER LAY-OUT	03/07/2001	WJV	WH	
01	CONTAINER LAY-OUT	27/06/2001	WJV	WH	
00	FIRST ISSUE	18/06/2001	WJV	WH	
REV.	DESCRIPTION:	DATE:	DRAWN:	CHECKED:	

CLIENT: **CDB ME RUBIN**

PROJECT: *SALVAGE MS KURSK*

TITLE: *DECK LAY OUT GIANT 4*

VAN SEUMEREN GROUP

MAMMOET

Karel Doormanweg 5, 3115 HK Schiedam, Harbour 550
P.O. Box 570, 3100 AN Schiedam, THE NETHERLANDS
Tel. +31(0)10-2042424 / Fax. +31(0)10-2042455
www.mammoet.com   engineering@nl.mammoet.com

DRAWING NUMBER

| SAP No: 500001660 | SCALE: 1/200 | SIZE: A1 | PROJECT No: P/103163 | DOC: -D- | PART: S21 | REV: -05 |

Sketches and Drawings

Strengthening Estimate Requirements from the Giant 4

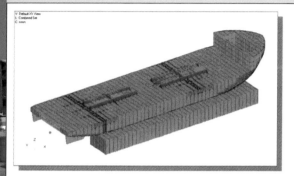

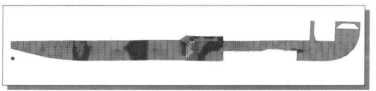

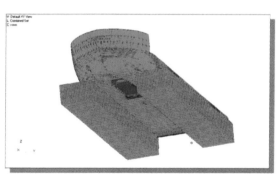

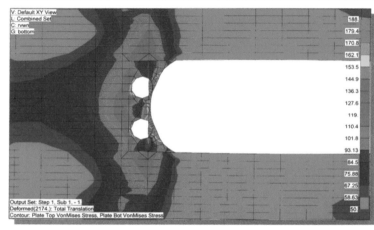

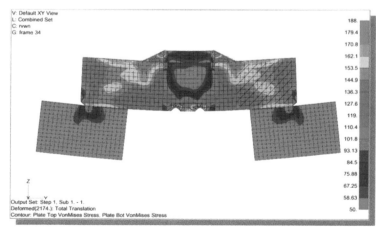

Sketches and Drawings

Cutaway Required from the Giant 4 for the conning-tower of The Kursk

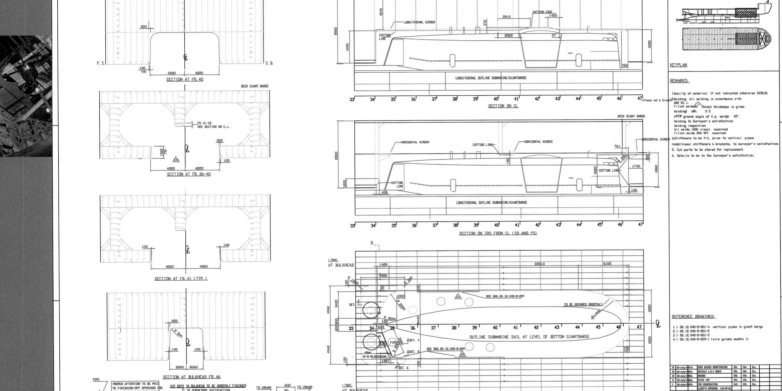

Sketches and Drawings

Lift Points and Pipes for the Grippers

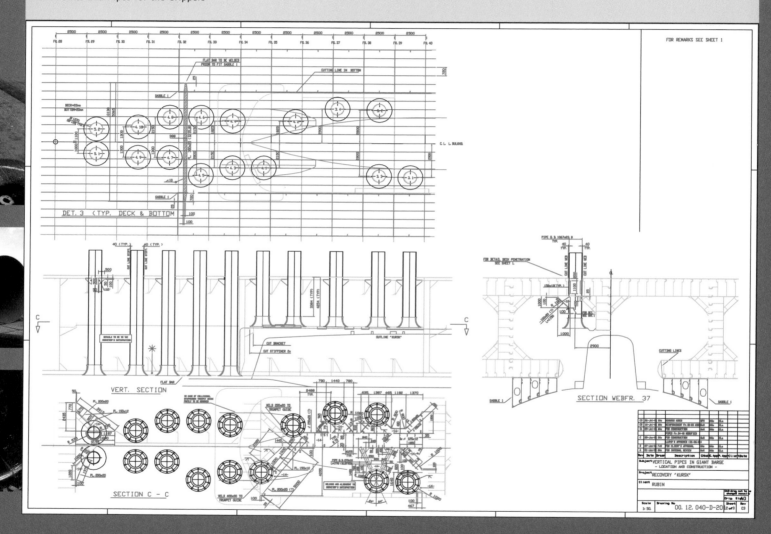

Sketches and Drawings

How the Strandjacks Operate

| Start situation | Lifting | Take over | Cylinder in | Next sequence |

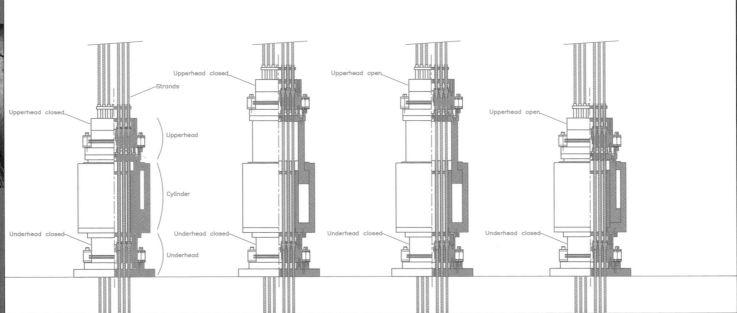

Upperhead closed
Strands
Upperhead closed
Upperhead
Cylinder
Underhead closed
Underhead

Upperhead closed
Underhead closed

Upperhead open
Underhead closed

Upperhead open
Underhead closed

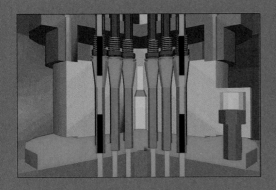

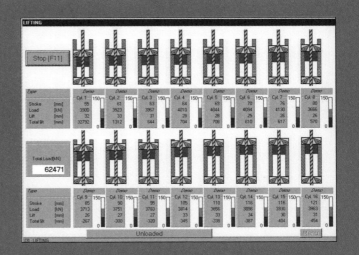

Sketches and Drawings

Klaas Lamphens First Sketch of the Strandjacks with the Heave Compensation System

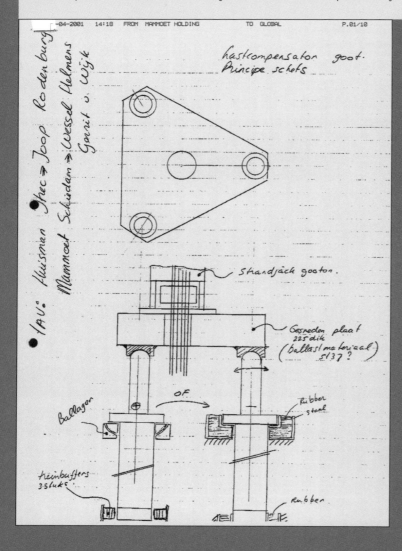

Sketches and Drawings

Klaas Lamphens Second Sketch of the Strandjacks with the Heave Compensation System

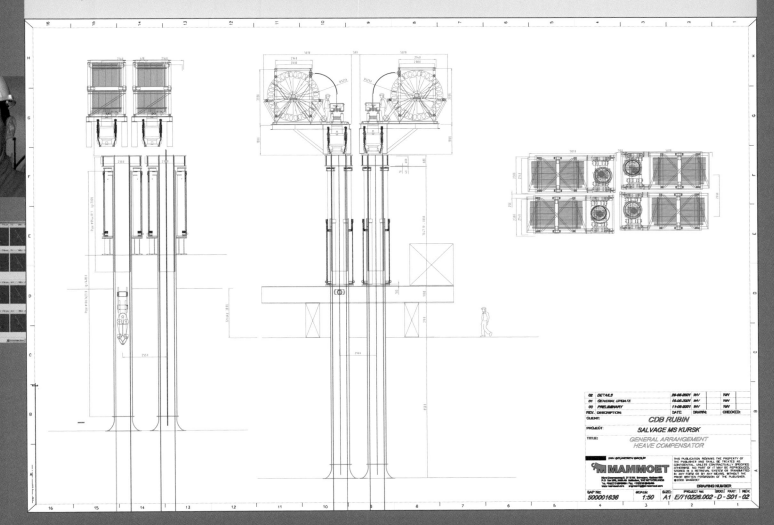

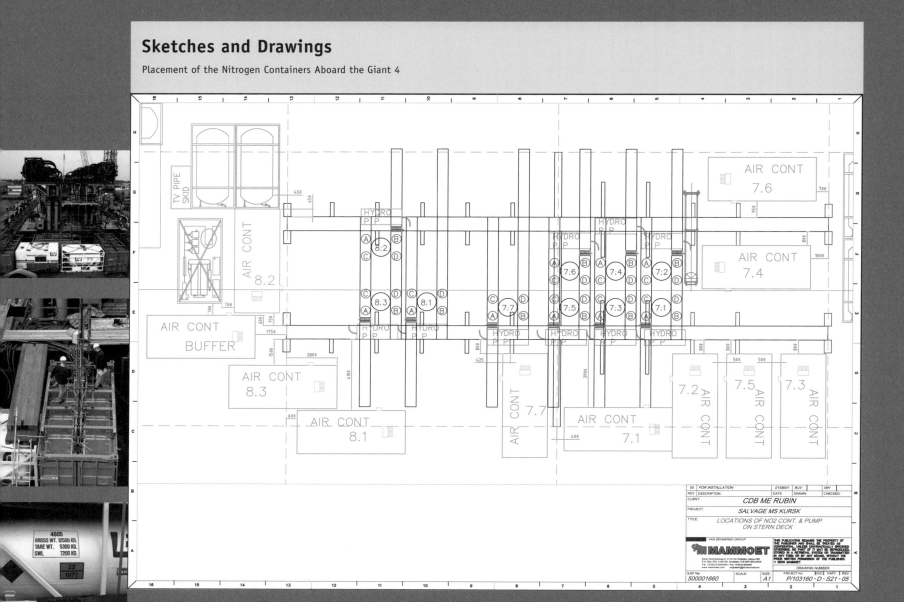

Sketches and Drawings

Placement of the Nitrogen Containers Aboard the Giant 4

Sketches and Drawings

Draft of the Winch Spools

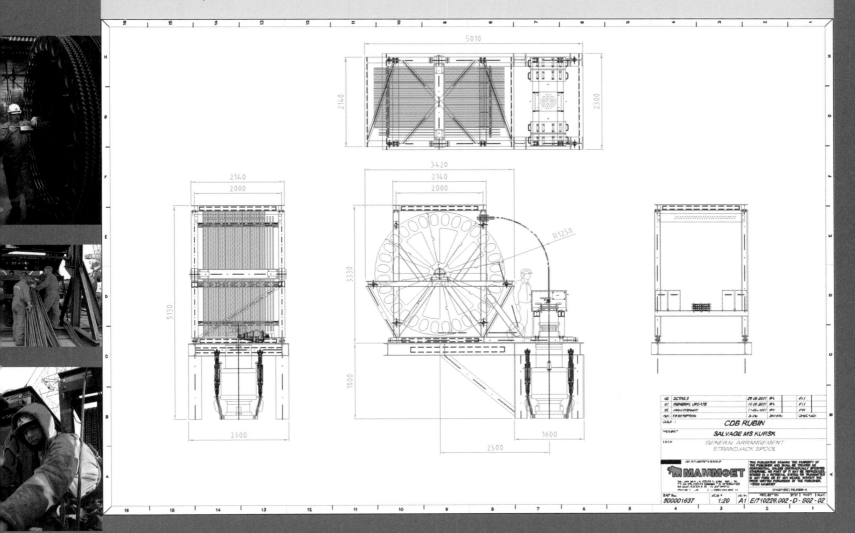

Sketches and Drawings

First Draft of the Grippers, Detailed Operational Drawing

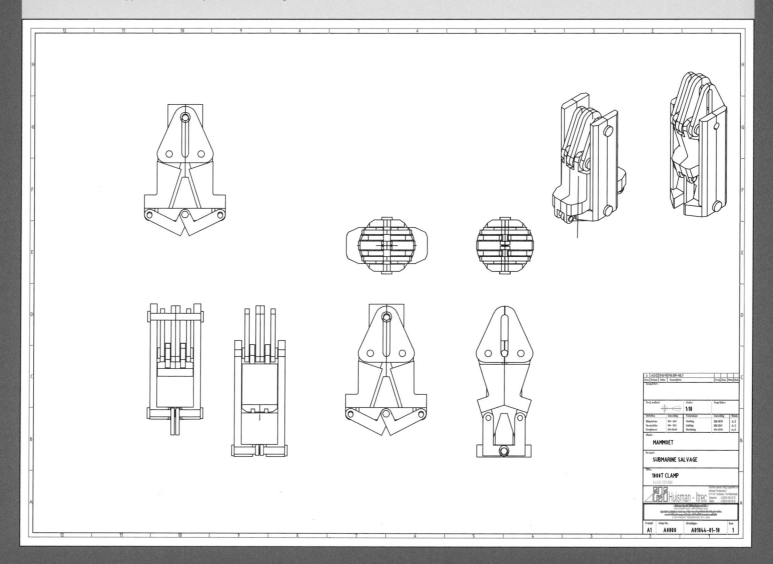

Sketches and Drawings

Final Draft of the Grippers, Complete Working Plan

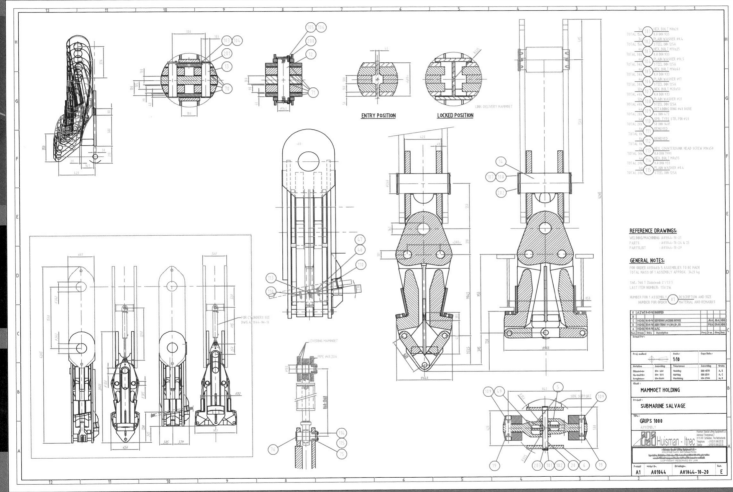

Sketches and Drawings

Gripper Strengthening Calculations

```
==========================================================================
    -280              +240          No Notch
    +440              +240          No Notch
==========================================================================
CALCULATION SHAFT                                           06-11-2001
==========================================================================
Surface pressure å-surf minimum :  -347  [N/mmý]
                  å-surf maximum :   347  [N/mmý]

Shear stress      1.00 * ç        minimum :  -147  [N/mmý]
                  1.00 * ç        maximum :   147  [N/mmý]
                          safety yield y : 2.74 [-]

Bending stress    1.00 * å-bend minimum :     0  [N/mmý]
                  1.00 * å-bend maximum :   258  [N/mmý]
                          safety yield y :  2.71 [-]
```

3.2.   Linkplates –2–

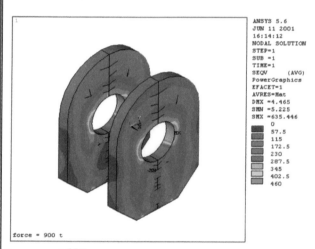

```
ANSYS 5.6
JUN 11 2001
16:14:12
NODAL SOLUTION
STEP=1
SUB =1
TIME=1
SEQV        (AVG)
PowerGraphics
EFACET=1
AVRES=Mat
DMX =4.465
SMN =5.225
SMX =635.446
        0
        57.5
        115
        172.5
        230
        287.5
        345
        402.5
        460
```

```
force = 900 t
```

Maximum stress: **635** mpa: (= 92% yield, ok StE 690)

3.   Calculations

3.1.   Link plate

Load equals 1000t /2 = 5000 kN.

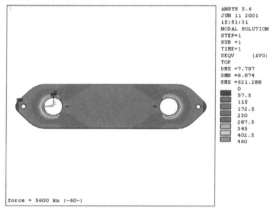

```
ANSYS 5.6
JUN 11 2001
15:51:31
NODAL SOLUTION
STEP=1
SUB =1
TIME=1
SEQV        (AVG)
TOP
DMX =7.797
SMN =9.874
SMX =621.288
        0
        57.5
        115
        172.5
        230
        287.5
        345
        402.5
        460
```

```
force = 5600 kn (-60-)
```

Maximum allowed force: 5600 kN. → 12% reserve.

```
Shaft
CALCULATION SHAFT                                           06-11-2001
──────────────────────────────────────────────────────────────────────
Input name of shaft : A01044 - Submarine

LOADING AND REACTIONS FOR SECTION FORCES                   06-11-2001
──────────────────────────────────────────────────────────────────────
Reactions
R(1) =  -5000.0 [kN]      xr(1) =  -250 [mm]       br(1) =  +60 [mm]
R(2) =  -5000.0 [kN]      xr(2) =  +250 [mm]       br(2) =  +60 [mm]

Loadings
F( 1)=  +5000.0 [kN]      x( 1) =  -180 [mm]       b( 1) =  +60 [mm]
F( 2)=  +5000.0 [kN]      x( 2) =  +180 [mm]       b( 2) =  +60 [mm]

GEOMETRY                                                    06-11-2001
──────────────────────────────────────────────────────────────────────
Material : 30CrNiMo8 Q&T                xmin :   -280 [mm]
    yield :   700 [N/mmý]               xmax :   +280 [mm]
Surface  : Unflattened                  D-in :     +0 [mm]

Location x          Diameter D       Notchtype  Notchrad/Peakfactor
    [mm]                [mm]             [-]          [mm]/[-]
```

Sketches and Drawings

First Sketch, Re-entry System (Small Illustration at Left Shows the Final Results)

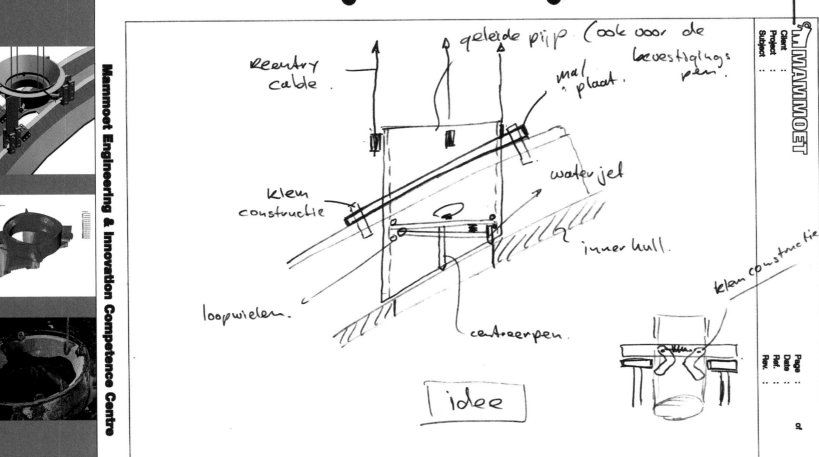

Sketches and Drawings

Cross-section of the Kursk

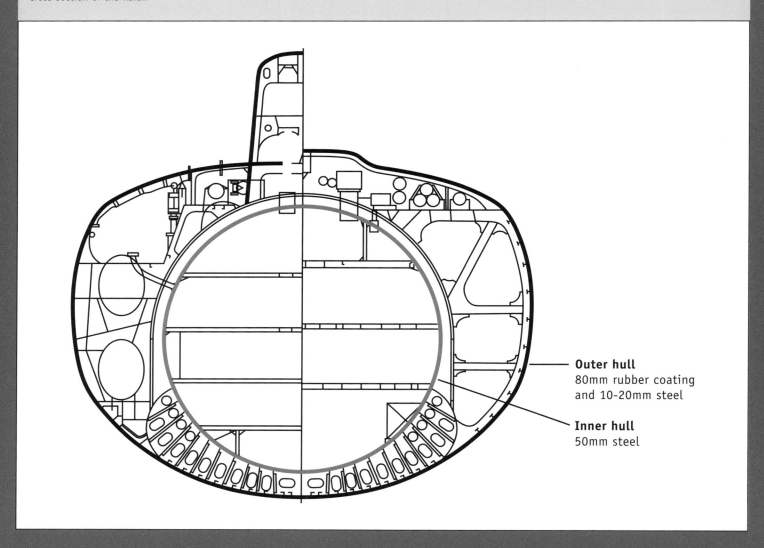

Outer hull
80mm rubber coating
and 10-20mm steel

Inner hull
50mm steel

Sketches and Drawings

Cross-section of the Kursk with the gripperguide installed on hole 8.1

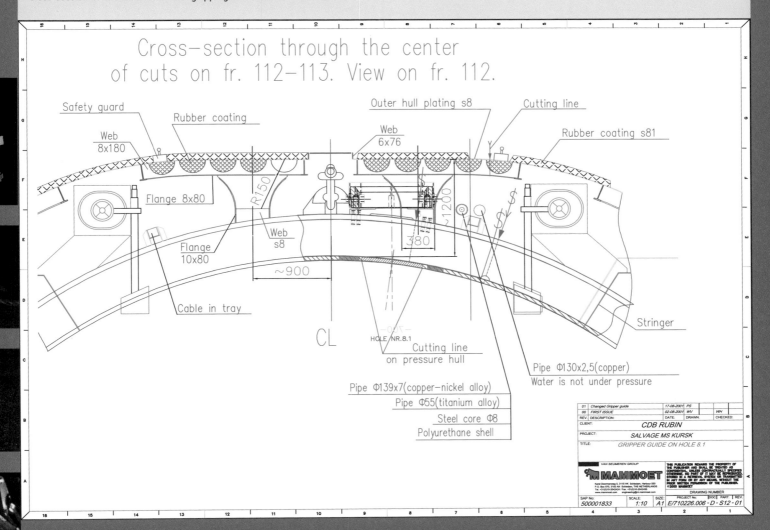

Cross—section through the center
of cuts on fr. 112—113. View on fr. 112.

Sketches and Drawings

Cross-section of the Kursk on the Saw Line

Fr. 16, looking forward

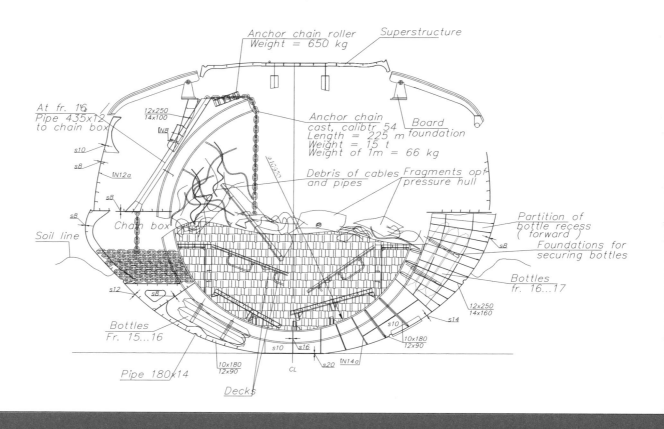

Sketches and Drawings

Operational Sketch of the Saw System

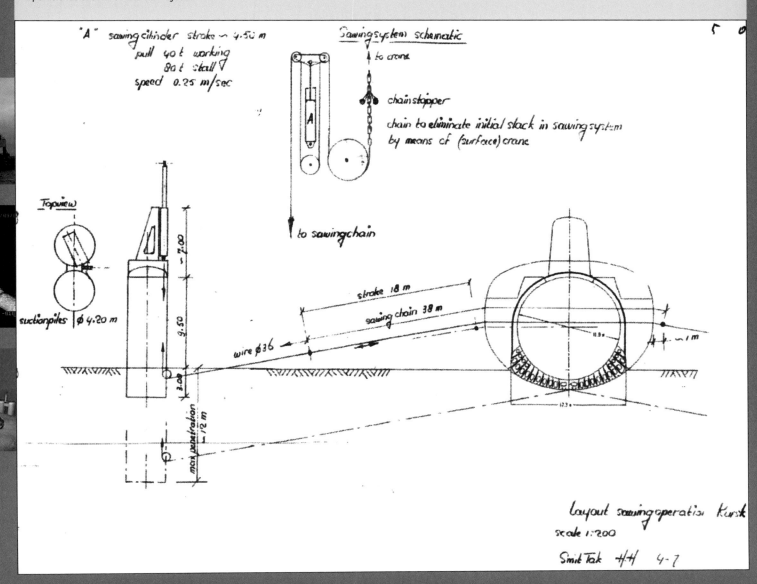

Sketches and Drawings

The Mooring of the Giant 4 on the Barentsz Sea

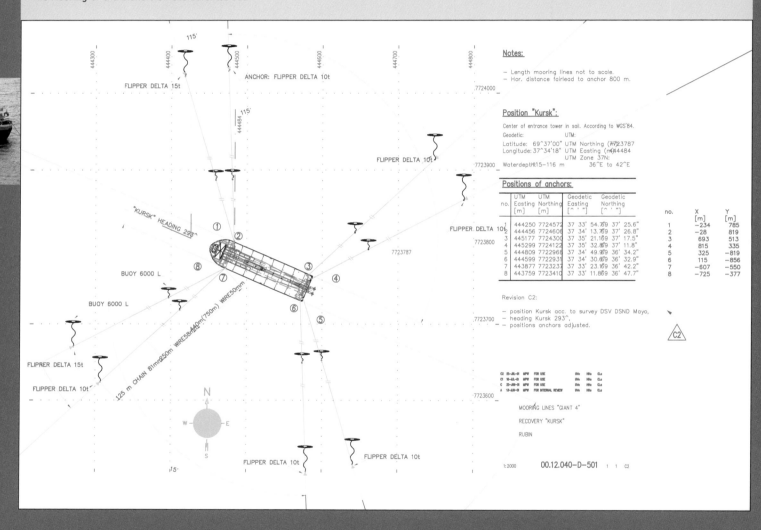

Notes:

- Length mooring lines not to scale.
- Hor. distance fairlead to anchor 800 m.

Position "Kursk":

Center of entrance tower in soil. According to WGS'84.

Geodetic: UTM:
Latitude: 69^37'00"   UTM Northing (m) 7723787
Longitude: 37^34'18"   UTM Easting (m) 444484
                         UTM Zone 37N:
Waterdepth: 115–116 m   36^E to 42^E

Positions of anchors:

no.	UTM Easting [m]	UTM Northing [m]	Geodetic Easting [^ ' "]	Geodetic Northing [^ ' "]	no.	X [m]	Y [m]
1	444250	7724572	37 33' 54.7"	69 37' 25.6"	1	−234	785
2	444456	7724606	37 34' 13.7"	69 37' 26.8"	2	−28	819
3	445177	7724300	37 35' 21.1"	69 37' 17.5"	3	693	513
4	445299	7724122	37 35' 32.8"	69 37' 11.8"	4	815	335
5	444809	7722968	37 34' 49.9"	69 36' 34.2"	5	325	−819
6	444599	7722931	37 34' 30.6"	69 36' 32.9"	6	115	−856
7	443877	7723237	37 33' 23.1"	69 36' 42.2"	7	−607	−550
8	443759	7723410	37 33' 11.8"	69 36' 47.7"	8	−725	−377

Revision C2:

- position Kursk acc. to survey DSV DSND Mayo,
- heading Kursk 293^,
- positions anchors adjusted.

C2

C2	25-JUL-01	MPW	FOR USE	GVn	HWe	CLe
C1	16-JUL-01	MPW	FOR USE	GVn	HWe	CLe
C	29-JAN-01	MPW	FOR USE	GVn	HWe	CLe
A	13-JUN-01	MPW	FOR INTERNAL REVIEW	GVn	HWe	CLe

MOORING LINES "GIANT 4"

RECOVERY "KURSK"

RUBIN

1:2000   00.12.040-D-501   1 1 C2

Sketches and Drawings

How the Kursk Hangs Under the Giant 4

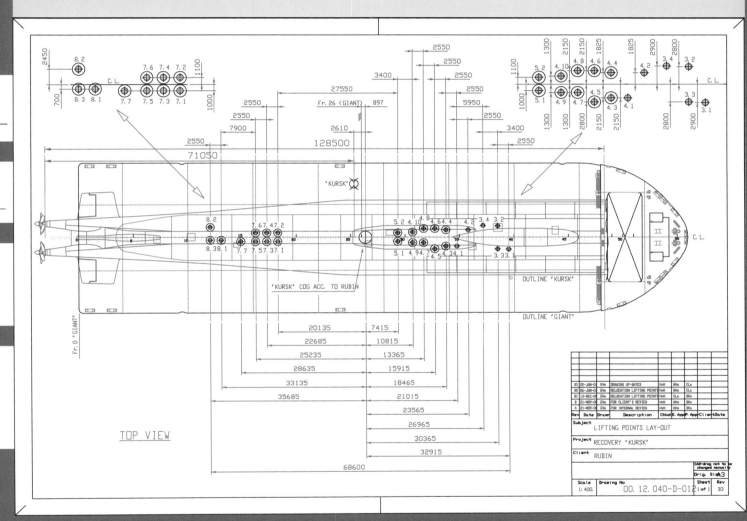

TOP VIEW

'KURSK'

'KURSK' COG ACC. TO RUBIN

OUTLINE 'KURSK'

OUTLINE 'GIANT'

Fr. 0 'GIANT'

Fr. 26 (GIANT)

C.L.

Subject	LIFTING POINTS LAY-OUT
Project	RECOVERY 'KURSK'
Client	RUBIN

| Scale | Drawing No | Sheet | Rev |
| 1:400. | 00.12.040-D-012 | 1 of 1 | B3 |

Sketches and Drawings

Cables for Measuring Radioactivity

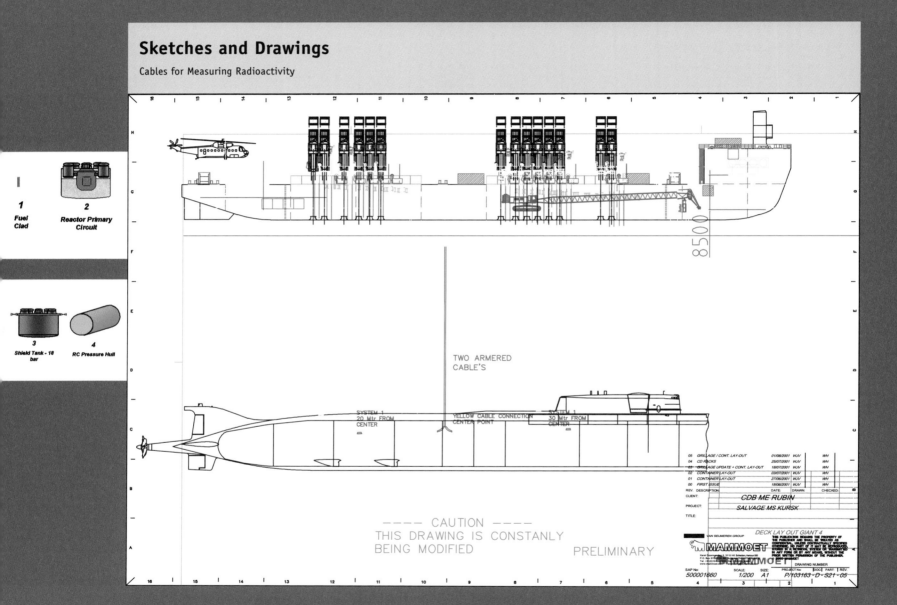

1
Fuel Clad

2
Reactor Primary Circuit

3
Shield Tank - 18 bar

4
RC Pressure Hull

TWO ARMERED CABLE'S

SYSTEM 1
20 Mtr FROM CENTER

YELLOW CABLE CONNECTION
CENTER POINT

SYSTEM 1
30 Mtr FROM CENTER

8500

05	GRILLAGE / CONT. LAY-OUT	01/08/2001	W./V	WH	
04	CD RACKS	25/07/2001	W./V	WH	
03	GRILLAGE UPDATE + CONT. LAY-OUT	18/07/2001	W./V	WH	
02	CONTAINER LAY-OUT	03/07/2001	W./V	WH	
01	CONTAINER LAY-OUT	27/06/2001	W./V	WH	
00	FIRST ISSUE	18/06/2001	W./V	WH	
REV:	DESCRIPTION:	DATE:	DRAWN:	CHECKED:	

CLIENT: CDB ME RUBIN

PROJECT: SALVAGE MS KURSK

TITLE: DECK LAY OUT GIANT 4

--- CAUTION ---
THIS DRAWING IS CONSTANLY
BEING MODIFIED   PRELIMINARY

MAMMOET
VAN SEUMEREN GROUP

| SAP No: | SCALE: | SIZE: | PROJECT No: | DOC: | PART: | REV: |
| 500001660 | 1/200 | A1 | P/103163–D–S21–05 | | | |

DRAWING NUMBER

Sketches and Drawings

The Position of the Pontoons Mar and Gon Under the Giant 4

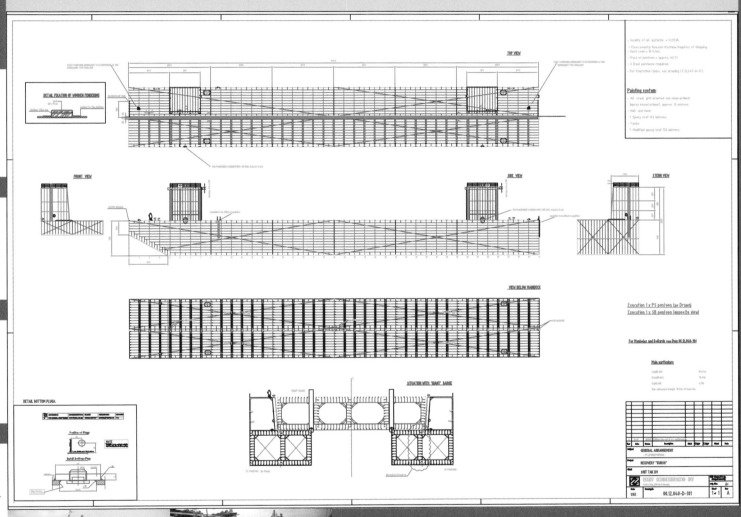

ABOUT THE AUTHOR

Hans Offringa (1956) is a publisher, media-advisor and writer/translator. Already in 1978 he specialized in electronic media and is internationally considered a pioneer in this field. Over the past 15 years he produced a series of educational television programs, wrote numerous articles on media and a variety of books, amongst which four drawing books and three novels. In 1996 he developed a new business model for the publishing industry which has become a business case in the Dutch edition of Philip Kotler's "Principles of Marketing."

Also an internationally acknowledged expert on Single Malt Whisky, Hans translated two Scottish whiskybooks into Dutch and recently finished writing a road-novel on Scotch and Scotland, that was published in the Netherlands by Spectrum in September 2004. He is a member of the Scotch Malt Whisky Society and consul of the world-famous whiskyhotel 'Craigellachie of Speyside'.

Since 2000/2001 Hans lectures at Erasmus University Rotterdam on publishing. When not travelling in Europe or the US for his publishing company, he spends time writing, doing whisky nosing & tastings for business clubs and restaurants or driving classic car rallys. He is the proud father of two sons and lives on the outskirts of an ancient town in the eastern part of the Netherlands.

www.hansoffringa.com